UML in Practice

UML in Practice

The Art of Modeling Software Systems Demonstrated through Worked Examples and Solutions

Pascal Roques

JOHN WILEY & SONS, LTD

Translation from the French language edition of: *UML par la pratique by Pascal Roques*
© 2001 Editions Eyrolles, Paris, France

Translation Copyright © 2004 John Wiley & Sons Ltd, The Atrium, Southern Gate,
Chichester, West Sussex PO19 8SQ, England
Telephone   (+44) 1243 779777

Email (for orders and customer service enquiries): cs-books@wiley.co.uk
Visit our Home Page on www.wileyeurope.com or www.wiley.com

Other Wiley Editorial Offices

John Wiley & Sons Inc., 111 River Street, Hoboken, NJ 07030, USA

Jossey-Bass, 989 Market Street, San Francisco, CA 94103-1741, USA

Wiley-VCH Verlag GmbH, Boschstr. 12, D-69469 Weinheim, Germany

John Wiley & Sons Australia Ltd, 33 Park Road, Milton, Queensland 4064, Australia

John Wiley & Sons (Asia) Pte Ltd, 2 Clementi Loop #02-01, Jin Xing Distripark, Singapore 129809

John Wiley & Sons Canada Ltd, 22 Worcester Road, Etobicoke, Ontario, Canada M9W 1L1

Wiley also publishes its books in a variety of electronic formats. Some content that appears in print may not be available in electronic books.

British Library Cataloguing in Publication Data

A catalogue record for this book is available from the British Library

ISBN 0-470-84831-6

Translated and Typeset by Cybertechnics Ltd, Sheffield
Printed and bound in Great Britain by Biddles Ltd, Kings Lynn
This book is printed on acid-free paper responsibly manufactured from sustainable forestry in which at least two trees are planted for each one used for paper production.

"A is a good model of B if satisfactory answers can be given by A to questions predefined on B."

Douglas T. Ross

"The difference between theory and practice is that in theory, there is no difference between theory and practice, but in practice, there is."

Jan van de Sneptscheut

"Since ancient times, man has searched for a language, which is both universal and synthetic. Their search led them to discover images, symbols that – by reducing them to the essential – express the richest and most complex realities. The images, the symbols speak – they have a language."

O.M. Aïvanhov

Contents

Foreword

The heart of the challenge in building software-intensive systems is complexity. Computers are universal machines, and as David Eck examined in *The Most Complex Machine*, software "machines" are the most complex things humans build. Compounding this is the many degrees of freedom we as software developers "enjoy" in building systems; there are so many algorithms, components, and ways of connecting things. No wonder we both suffer and delight in the creative opportunities of software development!

The essential weapons against this complexity are abstraction and decomposition. And abstraction is a function of our languages. Our language deeply influences our view. Choosing a spreadsheet language, dance, Java, or the UML to describe a problem and solution shapes how we think about it.

Research indicates that approximately 50% of the cerebral cortex in primates (including us) is involved in vision processing. Communicating and exploring with visual languages plays to a major strength of our brains. Size, spatial relationships, color contrasts, and so on are subconsciously processed with breathtaking speed, conveying much–and fast.

These facts should not be lost sight of in the on-going debates of the value of visual vs. textual programming languages. Textual code (e.g., Java source) is a very low level of abstraction, and does not leverage the natural strength of the human brain as an optimized system for visual analysis. My interest is not just to focus on useful code manipulation-optimizing techniques, such as Extreme Programming or IDEs with refactoring tools, but to find ways to understand and build software using more human-oriented languages, iconic and visual. Make computers understand languages our brains favor, not vice versa.

This is part of the vision of the UML. It isn't just about drawing sketches; it is a vision of tackling complexity and increasing abstraction with better human-oriented languages. Not an easy goal, but worthy. We can't achieve order-of-magnitude improvements in productivity with the current levels of abstraction offered by today's textual computer languages that are not substantively different than FORTRAN-54.

I know that my friend Pascal Roques shares this vision. And Pascal is involved in day-to-day software development. As such, he cares about the practical use of the UML to add value–not simply as an academic toy. Pascal is an expert developer, modeler, and a thoughtful and sensitive teacher. You can see this in his detailed discussion of the trade-offs in different solutions to the problems–it is a great educational contribution to see how a skilled modeler and designer sees alternatives, and makes choices.

By using this excellent book of UML examples and practice, you will gain much in understanding and becoming fluid in the UML. Enjoy!

Craig Larman

Bracebridge, Ontario

Dec 2003

www.craiglarman.com

Introduction

Aims of the book

For several years now, there has been a constant increase in the number of works on UML and object modelling. However, my practical experience of training (more than a thousand or so people trained in OMT, then UML since 1993...) convinced me that there is still another need that is not tended to by the multitude of books available at the moment: a book of marked exercises. In fact, during the seminars that I lead, I am devoting more and more time to discussion sessions with trainees on the compared merits of such or such modelling solution. Furthermore, I am firmly convinced that these interactive discussions on concrete topics have a far more lasting impact for them than the theoretical presentation of the subtleties of UML formalism!

This led me to form an extensive database of exercises, the majority of which have been taken from current or past training courses offered by the company of Valtech. I also drew my inspiration from core books, which have helped me to further my own knowledge of this subject, in particular that of J. Rumbaugh on OMT[1] (one of the first to suggest giving exercises after each introductory chapter on a topic) and the best seller of C. Larman[2] on object-oriented analysis and design.

It is this educational material, based on hours of enriching discussions with trainees from all backgrounds and abilities, that I would like to share with you today. From their questions and suggestions, they compelled me to take into account the most diverse points of view on the shared problem of modelling, as well as improve my argumentation and sometimes to envisage new solutions, to which I had not given any thought at all!

Prerequisites

The reader is assumed to have mastered the core concepts of the object-oriented approach (class, instance, encapsulation, inheritance, polymorphism), having had, for example, practical experience of an object-oriented programming language, such as C++ or Java.

---

1. *Object-Oriented Modeling and Design*, J. Rumbaugh et al., Prentice Hall, 1991.

2. *Applying UML and Patterns*, C. Larman, Prentice Hall, 1997.

For a complete overview of UML formalism, the reader will be able to refer to comprehensive manuals, such as:

- *The Unified Modeling Language User Guide*, G. Booch, Addison-Wesley, 1999;

- *The Unified Modeling Language Reference Manual*, J. Rumbaugh, Addison-Wesley, 1999;

- *UML Distilled: A Brief Guide to the Standard Object Modeling Language* (3rd Edition), M. Fowler, K. Scott, Addison-Wesley, 2003.

Note that the latest version of the UML Specifications can be found on the OMG web site (www.omg.org, or www.uml.org).

Layout of the book

To avoid confusing matters, the book is divided into parts in accordance with the three views of modelling: functional, static and dynamic, whilst emphasising for each the dominating UML diagram or diagrams (those which are not in parentheses on the next figure).

In order to make a second differentiation – this time between the levels of abstraction – a distinction has been made between:

- an "analysis" level comprising the functional view, as well as a subset of static and dynamic views, excluding the component, deployment and collaboration diagrams;

- a "design" view, which places emphasis on collaboration diagrams and the design detail of class diagrams, and which also introduces component and deployment diagrams.

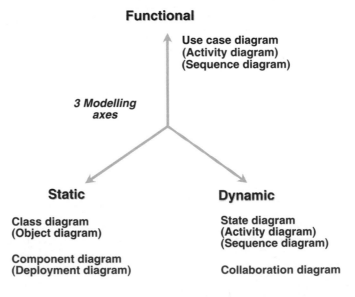

The first three parts of the book, therefore, each correspond to an analytical view of modelling, and the fourth part to design.

For each part, one main, specific case study acts as the first chapter. Complementary exercises can be found in the subsequent chapter.

A condensed table of contents is given below.

Part 1 Functional view

Chapter 1: Case study: ATM

Chapter 2: Complementary exercises

Appendix A: Glossary & tips

Part 2 Static view

Chapter 3: Case study: flight booking system

Chapter 4: Complementary exercises

Appendix B: Glossary & tips

Part 3 Dynamic view

Chapter 5: Case study: pay phone

Chapter 6: Complementary exercises

Appendix C: Glossary & tips

Part 4 Design

Chapter 7: Case study: training request

Chapter 8: Complementary exercises

Appendix D: Glossary & tips

Typographical conventions

In order to clarify matters somewhat whilst reading this book, the exercises and solutions are given prominence through the use of different character fonts and graphical symbols. Examples of these are given below:

Case study 1 – Problem statement

This case study concerns a simplified system of the automatic teller machine (ATM). The ATM offers the following services:

...

**   1.1   Identify the main actors of the ATM.

Answer 1.1

What are the external entities that interact directly with the ATM?

...

In order to guide the reader a little more, the level of difficulty of the questions is evaluated by assigning it between one and four stars:

*   : easy question,

**   : question of medium difficulty,

***   : fairly difficult question that involves some advanced concepts of UML,

****   : difficult question that requires complex argumentation.

Occasionally, in order to break up the monotony of the text, I have also used the following symbol to set apart a comment concerning a question of advanced level:

Graphical representations of an actor

The standard graphical representation of the actor in UML is the icon called *stick man*, with the name of the actor below the drawing. It is also possible to show an actor as a class rectangle, with the <<actor>> keyword. A third representation (halfway between the first two) is also possible, as indicated below:

...

Acknowledgements

This book would not have been able to see the light of day without agreement from the management of Valtech, who allowed me to utilise the material accumulated in the various training courses on UML which I have presented.

I am therefore eager to give special thanks to all those who have participated over the years in developing UML Valtech course support, such as Pierre Chouvalidzé, Thibault Cuvillier, Michel Ezran, Patrick Le Go, Franck Vallée, Philippe Riaux, Philippe Dubosq, Yann Le Tanou, Françoise Caron, Christophe Addinquy, etc., without forgetting our American colleagues, in particular, Craig Larman, Ken Howard and Chris Jones.

I would also like to thank all those whose discussions, comments and suggestions led me to improve my argumentation. First and foremost, I think of my numerous trainees, as well as my correspondents during consultancy work on the introduction of UML in various projects.

Thanks also to Éric Sulpice of Éditions Eyrolles for expressing renewed confidence, and especially for knowing how to motivate me by suggesting that I write this book of marked exercises.

Finally, a big thank you to Sylvie, who supported me for this English edition by her loving encouragements.

Part 1

Functional view

Case study: automatic teller machine

Aims of the chapter

By means of the first case study, this chapter will allow us to illustrate the main difficulties step by step, which are connected to implementing the technique of use cases.

Once we have identified the actors that interact with the system, we will develop our first UML model at a system level, in order to be able to establish precisely the boundaries of the system.

We will then learn how to identify use cases, and how to construct use case diagrams linking actors and use cases. Then we will see how to specify the functional view by explaining in detail the different ways in which actors can use the system. For this goal, we will learn to write textual descriptions as well as to draw complementary UML diagrams (such as sequence or activity diagrams).

Elements involved

- Actor

- Static context diagram

- Use case

- Use case diagram

- Primary actor, secondary actor

- Textual description of a use case

- Scenario, sequence

- System sequence diagram

- Activity diagram

- Inclusion, extension and generalisation of use cases
- Packaging use cases.

Case study 1 – Problem statement

This case study concerns a simplified system of the automatic teller machine (ATM). The ATM offers the following services:

1. Distribution of money to every holder of a smartcard via a card reader and a cash dispenser.
2. Consultation of account balance, cash and cheque deposit facilities for bank customers who hold a smartcard from their bank.

Do not forget either that:

3. All transactions are made secure.
4. It is sometimes necessary to refill the dispenser, etc.

From these four sentences, we will work through the following activities:

- Identify the actors,
- Identify the use cases,
- Construct a use case diagram,
- Write a textual description of the use cases,
- Complete the descriptions with dynamic diagrams,
- Organise and structure the use cases.

Watch out: the preceding problem statement is deliberately incomplete and imprecise, just as it is in real projects!

Note also that the problem and its solution are based on French banking systems and the use of smartcards: the system you actually use in your country may be significantly different! It is not very important. What is important is the way of thinking to solve this functional problem as well as the UML concepts and diagrams that we use.

1.1 Step 1 – Identifying the actors of the ATM

First, we will identify the actors of the ATM system.

An actor is a construct employed in use cases that define a role that a user or any other system plays when interacting with the system under consideration. It is a type of entity that interacts, but which is itself external to the subject. Actors may represent human users, external hardware, or other subjects. An actor does not necessarily represent a specific physical entity. For instance, a single physical entity may play the role of several different actors and, conversely, a given actor may be played by multiple physical entities.[3]

** 1.1 Identify the main actors of the ATM.

Answer 1.1

What are the external entities that interact directly with the ATM?

Let's look at each of the sentences of the exposition in turn.

Sentence 1 allows us to identify an obvious initial actor straight away: every "holder of a smartcard". He or she will be able to use the ATM to withdraw money using his or her smartcard.

However, be careful: the card reader and cash dispenser constitute part of the ATM. They can therefore not be considered as actors! You can note down that the identification of actors requires the boundary between the system being studied and its environment to be set out exactly. If we restrict the study to the control/command system of physical elements of the ATM, the card reader and cash dispenser then become actors.

Another trap: is the smartcard itself an actor? The card is certainly external to the ATM, and it interacts with it... Yet, we do not recommend that you list it as an actor, as we are putting into practice the following principle: eliminate "physical" actors as much as possible to the advantage of "logical" actors. The actor is the who or what that benefits from using the system. It is the card holder who withdraws money to spend it, not the card itself!

Sentence 2 identifies additional services that are only offered to bank customers who hold a smartcard from this bank. This is therefore a different profile from the previous one, which we will realise by a second actor called *Bank customer*.

Sentence 3 encourages us to take into account the fact that all transactions are made secure. But who makes them secure? There are therefore other external entities, which play the role of authorisation system and with which the ATM

---

3. From the OMG document: "Unified Modeling Language: Superstructure (version 2.0)".

communicates directly. An interview with the domain expert[4] is necessary to allow us to identify two different actors:

- the Visa authorisation system (VISA AS) for withdrawal transactions carried out using a Visa smartcard (we restrict the ATM to Visa smartcards for reasons of simplification);

- the information system of the bank (Bank IS) to authorise all transactions carried out by a customer using his or her bank smartcard, but also to access the account balance.

Finally, sentence 4 reminds us that an ATM also requires maintenance work, such as refilling the dispenser with bank notes, retrieving cards that have been swallowed, etc. These maintenance tasks are carried out by a new actor, which – to simplify matters – we will call *Maintenance operator*.

Graphical representations of an actor

The standard graphical representation of the actor in UML is the icon called *stick man* with the name of the actor below the drawing. It is also possible to show an actor as a class rectangle with the <<actor>> keyword. A third representation (halfway between the first two) is also possible, as indicated below.

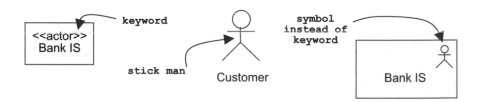

Figure 1.1 Possible graphical representations of an actor

A good piece of advice consists in using the graphical form of the *stick man* for human actors and that of the first rectangular representation for connected systems.

4. Remember that the domain refers to French banking systems, which may explain differences with your own knowledge and experience.

Rather than simply depicting the list of actors as in the previous figure, which does not provide any additional information with regard to a textual list, we can draw a diagram that we will call *static context diagram*. To do this, simply use a class diagram in which each actor is linked to a central class representing the system by an association, which enables the number of instances of actors connected to the system at a given time to be specified.

Even though this is not a traditional UML diagram, we have found this kind of "context diagram" very useful in our practical experience.

** 1.2 Map out the static context diagram of the ATM.

Answer 1.2

The ATM is fundamentally a single user system: at any moment, there is only one instance of each actor (at the most) connected to the system.

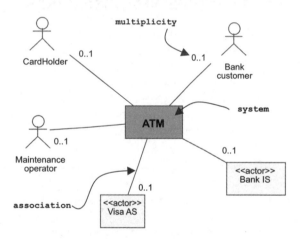

Figure 1.2 Static context diagram of the ATM

We should really add a graphical note to indicate that the human actors, *Bank customer* and *CardHolder* are, furthermore, mutually exclusive, which is not implicit according to the multiplicities of the associations.

Another solution, which is a little more developed, consists in considering *Bank customer* as a specialisation of *CardHolder*, as illustrated in the following figure. The aforementioned problem of exclusivity is therefore solved by adding an extra detail to the diagram.

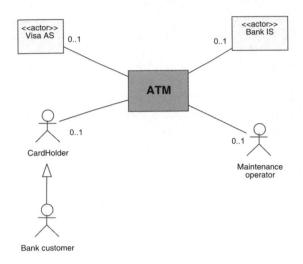

Figure 1.3 A more developed version of the static context diagram of the ATM

1.2   Step 2 – Identifying use cases

We are now going to identify the use cases.

A *use case* represents the specification of a sequence of actions, including variants, that a system can perform, interacting with actors of the system.[5]

A use case models a service offered by the system. It expresses the actor/system interactions and yields an observable result of value to an actor.

For each actor identified previously, it is advisable to search for the different business goals, according to which is using the system.

**   1.3   Prepare a preliminary list of use cases of the ATM, in order of actor.

Answer 1.3

Let's take the five actors one by one and list the different ways in which they can use the ATM:
CardHolder:

- Withdraw money.

---

5.   From the OMG document: "Unified Modeling Language: Superstructure (version 2.0)".

Bank customer:

- Withdraw money (something not to forget!).

- Consult the balance of one or more accounts.

- Deposit cash.

- Deposit cheques.

Maintenance operator:

- Refill dispenser.

- Retrieve cards that have been swallowed.

- Retrieve cheques that have been deposited.

Visa authorisation system (AS):

- None.

Bank information system (IS):

- None.

Primary or secondary actor

Contrary to what we might believe, all actors do not necessarily use the system! We call the one for whom the use case produces an observable result the *primary* actor. In contrast, *secondary* actors constitute the other participants of the use case.[6] Secondary actors are requested for additional information; they can only consult or inform the system when the use case is being executed.

This is exactly the case of the two "non-human" actors in our example: the *Visa AS* and the *Bank IS* are only requested by the ATM within the context of realising certain use cases. However, they themselves do not have their own way of using the ATM.

---

6. In his excellent book, *Writing Effective Use Cases* (Addison-Wesley, 2001), A. Cockburn defines similarly *supporting actors*: "A supporting actor in a use case is an external actor that provides a service to the system under design."

1.3   Step 3 – Creating use case diagrams

We are now going to give concrete expression to our identification of use cases by realising UML diagrams, aptly called use case diagrams. A use case diagram shows the relationships among actors and the subject (system), and use cases.

We can easily obtain a preliminary diagram by copying out the previous answer on a diagram that shows the use cases (ellipses) inside the ATM system (box) and linked by associations (lines) to their primary actors (the "stick man" icon).

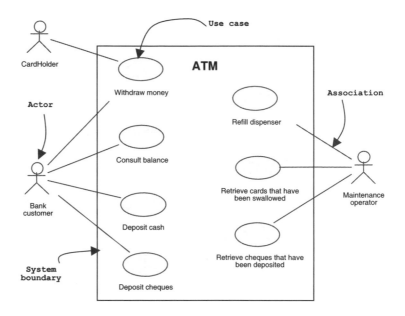

Figure 1.4   Preliminary use case diagram of the ATM

***   1.4   Propose another, more sophisticated version of this preliminary use case diagram.

Answer 1.4

The *Withdraw money* use case has two possible primary actors (but they cannot be simultaneous). Another way to express this notion is to consider the *Bank customer* actor as a specialisation (in the sense of the inheritance relationship) of the more general *CardHolder* actor. A bank customer is actually a particular card holder who has all the privileges of the latter, as well as others that are specific to him or her as a customer.

UML enables the depiction of a generalisation/specialisation relationship between actors, as indicated on the diagram below.

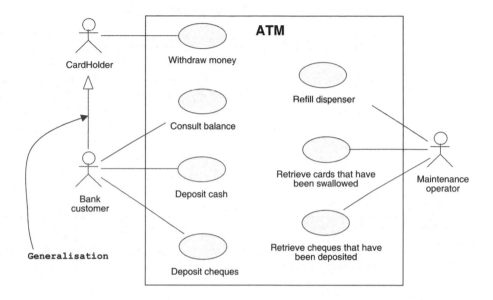

Figure 1.5 A more sophisticated version of the preliminary use case diagram

However, the significance of this generalisation relationship is not evident in our example. Certainly, it enables the association between the *Bank customer* actor and the *Withdraw money* use case to be removed, which is now inherited from the *CardHolder* actor, but on the other hand, it adds the symbol for generalisation between the two actors... Moreover, we will see in the following paragraph that the requested secondary actors are not the same in the case of the CardHolder and in that of the bank customer.

We will therefore not use this solution and, to reinforce this choice, we will rename the primary actor *Visa CardHolder*, to clarify matters a little more.

We now have to add the secondary actors in order to complete the use case diagram. To do this, we will simply make these actors appear with additional associations towards the existing use case.

Graphical precisions on the use case diagram

As far as we are concerned, we recommend that you adopt the following conventions in order to improve the informative content of these diagrams:

- by default, the role of an actor is "primary"; if this is not the case, indicate explicitly that the role is "secondary" on the association to the side of the actor;

- as far as possible, place the primary actors to the left of the use cases and the secondary actors to the right.

** 1.5 Complete the preliminary use case diagram by adding the secondary actors. To simplify matters, leave out the maintenance operator for the time being.

Answer 1.5

For all use cases appropriate for the bank customer, you must explicitly bring in *Bank IS* as a secondary actor.

But a problem arises for the shared use case, *Withdraw money*. Indeed, if the primary actor is a Visa card holder, the *Visa AS* must be called on (which will then be responsible for contacting the IS of the holder's bank); whereas the ATM will contact the *Bank IS* directly if it concerns a bank customer.[7]

One solution consists in adding an association with each of the two non-human actors. This simplistic modelling does not make it clear to the reader of the diagram that the actors are selectively participating two by two and not all together.

---

7. Remember that the domain refers to French banking systems, which may explain differences with your knowledge and experience.

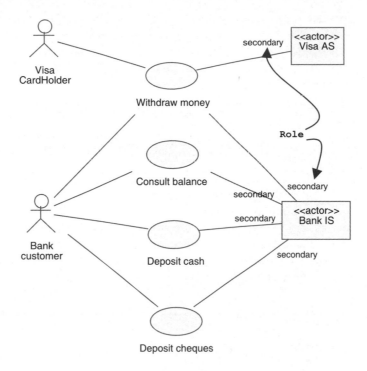

Figure 1.6 Simple version of the completed use case diagram

Another solution would be to distinguish two use cases for the withdrawal of money: *Withdraw money using a Visa card* and *Withdraw money using a bank card*. This more precise, yet more cumbersome, modelling is easier for the reader of the diagram to grasp. Furthermore, it clearly tells against the use of generalisation between actors, which was mentioned beforehand. Indeed, the distinction between the two use cases is contradictory with the attempt at inheritance of the unique *Withdraw money* case, which had been viewed more highly, while the secondary actors had not yet been added. We will keep this second solution for the follow-up to the exercise.

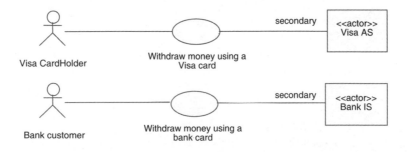

Figure 1.7 Fragment of the more precise version of the completed use case diagram

We will note that the *Bank IS* is not a direct actor of the *Withdraw money using a Visa card* use case, as we are considering that the *Visa AS* is taking upon itself to contact it, outside of reach of the ATM system. Obviously, if the bank issue money to a Visa customer, they need to claim this money back from Visa. We assume this is out of scope.

1.4 Step 4 – Textual description of use cases

Once the use cases have been identified, you then have to describe them!

In order to explain the dynamics of a use case in detail, the most obvious way of going about it involves textually compiling a list of all the interactions between the actors and the system. The use case must have a clearly identifiable beginning and end. The possible variants must also be specified, such as the main success scenario, alternative sequences, error sequences, whilst simultaneously trying to arrange the descriptions in a sequential order in order to improve their readability.

Scenarios and use cases

We call each unit of description of action sequences a *sequence*. A *scenario* represents a particular succession of sequences, which is run from beginning to end of the use case. A scenario may be used to illustrate an interaction or the execution of a use case instance.[8]

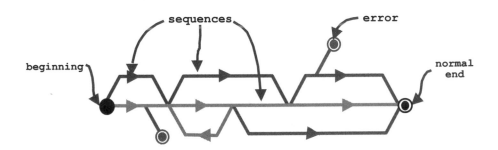

Figure 1.8 Representation of the scenarios of a use case

---

8.   From the OMG document: "Unified Modeling Language: Superstructure (version 2.0)".

The textual description record of a use case is not standardised by UML.[9] For our part, we recommend the following structuring:

Identification summary (mandatory)

- includes title, summary, creation and modification dates, version, person in charge, actors...

Flow of events (mandatory)

- describes the main success scenario,[10] the alternative and error sequences,[11] as well as the preconditions and the postconditions.

UI requirements (optional)

- possibly adds graphical user interface constraints (required look and feel). Screen copies, indeed a disposable model, are greatly appreciated.

Non-functional constraints (optional)

- may possibly add the following information: frequency, availability, accuracy, integrity, confidentiality, performance, concurrency, etc.

**   1.6   Describe the mandatory part of the *withdraw money using a visa card* use case.

Answer 1.6

Identification summary

Title: Withdraw money using a Visa card

Summary: this use case allows a Visa card holder, who is not a customer of the bank, to withdraw money if his or her daily limit allows it.

---

9.   You can find use case templates on the Web, for instance on www.usecases.org.

10.   The main success scenario is also known as "basic flow of events" or "normal path".

11.   The distinction we make is that with an alternative scenario, the primary actor achieves his or her goal, even though with an error one, the actor's goal is not achieved and the use case fails.

Actors: Visa CardHolder (primary), Visa AS (secondary).

Creation date: 02/03/02   **Date of update:** 08/19/03

Version: 2.2   **Person in charge:** Pascal Roques

Flow of events

Preconditions:

- The ATM cash box is well stocked.

- There is no card in the reader.

Main success scenario:

1. The Visa CardHolder inserts his or her smartcard in the ATM's card reader.
2. The ATM verifies that the card that has been inserted is indeed a smartcard.
3. The ATM asks the Visa CardHolder to enter his or her pin number.
4. The Visa CardHolder enters his or her pin number.
5. The ATM compares the pin number with the one that is encoded on the chip of the smartcard.[12]
6. The ATM requests an authorisation from the VISA authorisation system.
7. The VISA authorisation system confirms its agreement and indicates the daily withdrawal limit.
8. The ATM asks the Visa CardHolder to enter the desired withdrawal amount.
9. The Visa CardHolder enters the desired withdrawal amount.
10. The ATM checks the desired amount against the daily withdrawal limit.
11. The ATM asks the Visa CardHolder if he or she would like a receipt.
12. The Visa CardHolder requests a receipt.
13. The ATM returns the card to the Visa CardHolder.
14. The Visa CardHolder takes his or her card.
15. The ATM issues the banknotes and a receipt.
16. The Visa CardHolder takes the banknotes and the receipt.

---

12. Remember that the use case assumes smartcards, which contain the PIN, contrarily to "ordinary" cards with a magnetic stripe on the back as in North America.

Another possible presentation[13] consists in separating the actions of the actors and those of the system into two columns as follows:

1. The Visa CardHolder inserts his or her card in the ATM's card reader.	2. The ATM verifies that the card that has been inserted is indeed a Visa card.
	3. The ATM asks the Visa CardHolder to enter his or her pin number.
4. The Visa CardHolder enters his or her pin number.	5. The ATM compares the pin number with the one that is encoded on the chip of the card.
	6. The ATM requests an authorisation from the VISA authorisation system.
7. The VISA authorisation system confirms its agreement and indicates the daily balance.	8. The ATM asks the Visa CardHolder to enter the desired withdrawal amount.
9. The Visa CardHolder enters the desired withdrawal amount.	10. The ATM checks the desired amount against the daily balance.
	11. The ATM asks the Visa CardHolder if he or she would like a receipt.
12. The Visa CardHolder requests a receipt.	13. The ATM returns the card to the Visa CardHolder.
14. The Visa CardHolder takes his or her card.	15. The ATM issues the notes and a receipt.
16. The Visa CardHolder takes the notes and the receipt.	

"Alternative" sequences:

A1: *temporarily incorrect pin number*
The A1 sequence starts at point 5 of the main success scenario.

6.   The ATM informs the CardHolder that the pin is incorrect for the first or second time.

7.   The ATM records the failure on the smartcard.

---

13.   This presentation option was recommended by C. Larman in the first version of his book: *Applying UML and Patterns*, Prentice Hall, 1997.

The scenario goes back to point 3.

A2: the amount requested is greater than the daily withdrawal limit
The A2 sequence starts at point 10 of the main success scenario.

11. The ATM informs the CardHolder that the amount requested is greater than the daily withdrawal limit.

The scenario goes back to point 8.

A3: the Visa CardHolder does not want a receipt
The A3 sequence starts at point 11 of the main success scenario.

12. The Visa CardHolder declines the offer of a receipt.

13. The ATM returns the smartcard to the Visa CardHolder.

14. The Visa CardHolder takes his or her smartcard.

15. The ATM issues the banknotes.

16. The Visa CardHolder takes the banknotes.

Error sequences:

E1: invalid card
The E1 sequence starts at point 2 of the main success scenario.

3. The ATM informs the Visa CardHolder that the smartcard is not valid (unreadable, expired, etc.) and confiscates it; the use case fails.

E2: conclusively incorrect pin number
The E2 sequence starts at point 5 of the main success scenario.

6. The ATM informs the Visa CardHolder that the pin is incorrect for the third time.

7. The ATM confiscates the smartcard.

8. The VISA authorisation system is notified; the use case fails.

E3: unauthorised withdrawal
The E3 sequence starts at point 6 of the main success scenario.

7. The VISA authorisation system forbids any withdrawal.

8. The ATM ejects the smartcard; the use case fails.

E4: the card is not taken back by the holder
The E4 sequence starts at point 13 of the main success scenario.

14. After 15 seconds, the ATM confiscates the smartcard.

15. The VISA authorisation system is notified; the use case fails.

E5: the banknotes are not taken by the holder
The E5 sequence starts at point 15 of the main success scenario.

16. After 30 seconds, the ATM takes back the banknotes.

17. The VISA authorisation system is informed; the use case fails

Postconditions:

- The cashbox of the ATM contains fewer notes than it did at the start of the use case (the number of notes missing depends on the withdrawal amount).

*   1.7   Complete the description of the *withdraw money using a visa card* use case with the two optional paragraphs. Assume for instance that the new system must run on existing ATM hardware.

Answer 1.7

UI requirements

The input/output mechanisms available to the Visa CardHolder must be:

- A smartcard reader.

- A numerical keyboard (to enter his or her pin number), with "enter", "correct" and "cancel" keys.

- A screen to display any messages from the ATM.

- Keys around the screen so that the card holder can select a withdrawal amount from the amounts that are offered.

- A note dispenser.

- A receipt dispenser.

Non-functional constraints

Constraints	Specifications
Response time	The interface of the ATM must respond within a maximum time limit of 2 seconds. A nominal withdrawal transaction must take less than 2 minutes.
Concurrency	Non applicable (single user).
Availability	The ATM can be accessed 24/7.[14] A lack of paper for the printing of receipts must not prevent the card holder from being able to withdraw money.
Integrity	The interfaces of the ATM must be extremely sturdy to avoid vandalism.
Confidentiality	The procedure of comparing the pin number that has been entered on the keyboard of the ATM with that of the smartcard must have a maximum failure rate of 10^{-6}.

1.5   Step 5 – Graphical description of use cases

The textual description is essential for the documentation of use cases, as it alone enables ease of communication with users, as well as agreeing on domain terminology that is used.

However, the text also has its disadvantages as it difficult to show how the sequences follow one another, or at what moment the secondary actors are requested. Besides, keeping a record of changes often turns out to be rather tiresome. It is therefore recommended to complete the textual description with one or more dynamic UML diagrams.

---

14. This non-functional requirement is here as an example, but should be removed in the end and put at the system level as it applies to all use cases.

Dynamic descriptions of a use case

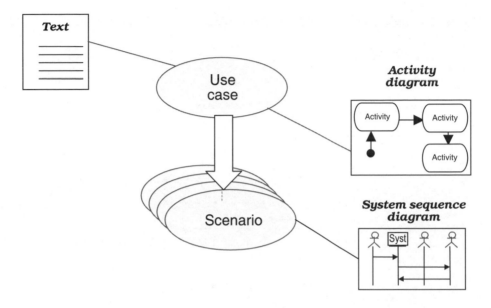

Figure 1.9   UML diagrams that we recommmend for completing the description of a use case

- For use cases, we recommend the *activity diagram,* as users find it far easier to understand since it resembles a traditional diagram. However, the *state diagram* may be useful for use cases that are very interactive.

- For certain scenarios, the *sequence diagram* works well. We recommend that you present it by showing the primary actor on the left, then an object representing the system in a black box, and finally, any secondary actors that may be requested during the scenario on the right of the system. We will use the title *system sequence diagram* as proposed by Larman.[15]

15.   Refer to *Applying UML and Patterns* (2nd Edition), Prentice-Hall, 2001.

*   1.8   Create a system sequence diagram that describes the main success scenario of
               the *Withdraw money using a Visa card* use case.

Answer 1.8

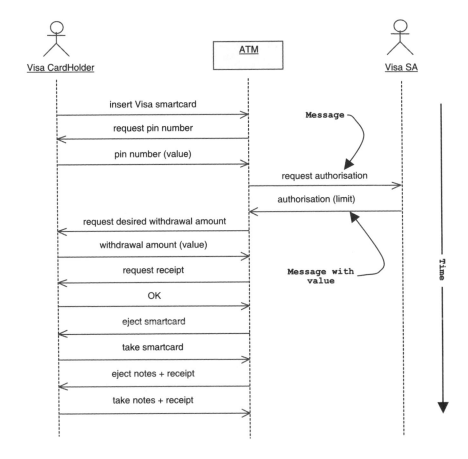

Figure 1.10   System sequence diagram of the "Withdraw money using a Visa card" main
success scenario

All you need to do is copy the interactions quoted in the textual scenario of answer
1.6 into a sequence diagram by following the graphical conventions listed above:

• the primary actor, Visa CardHolder, on the left,

- an object representing the ATM system as a whole in the middle,

- the secondary actor, Visa AS, to the right of the ATM.

Unlike the previous sequence diagram that only describes the main success scenario, the activity diagram can represent all the activities that are carried out by the system, with all the conditional branches and all the possible loops.

The activity diagram is essentially a flowchart, showing flow of control from activity to activity. The transitions are triggered at the end of activities or actions; steps can be carried out in parallel or in sequence.

Activity state or action state

An *activity state* models the realisation of an activity that:

- is complex and can be broken down into activities or actions,

- can be interrupted by an event.

An *action state* models the realisation of an action that:

- is simple and cannot be broken down,

- is atomic, which cannot be interrupted.

***   1.9   Construct an activity diagram that describes the dynamics of the *withdraw money using a visa card* use case.

Answer 1.9

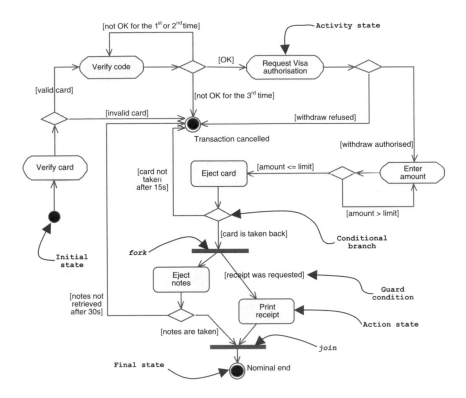

Figure 1.11 Activity diagram of Withdraw money using a Visa card

Note that the activity diagram differs slightly from the text: it omits the step to ask if a receipt is wanted, as we did not want to clutter the diagram. But the result of the step is nonetheless taken into account by the guard condition labelled "receipt was requested".

Additions to the system sequence diagram

A possibility that meets halfway consists in expanding the system sequence diagram of the nominal scenario in order to introduce the following:

- the main internal activities of the system (by means of messages that it sends to itself),

- references to "alternative" and error sequences (by means of notes).

This often results in a diagram that is less complex to read than an activity diagram, as there are fewer symbols, but it nevertheless retains an informative content for the specialist.

** 1.10 Expand the system sequence diagram that describes the nominal scenario of the *Withdraw money using a visa card* use case.

Answer 1.10

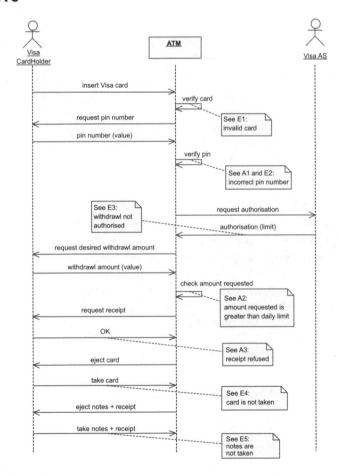

Figure 1.12 Expanded system sequence diagram of the Withdraw money using a Visa card main success scenario

1.6   Step 6 – Organising the use cases

In this final stage, we will refine our diagrams and descriptions.

With UML, it is actually possible to detail and organise use cases in two different and complementary ways:

- by adding include, extend and generalisation relationships between use cases;

- by grouping them into packages to define functional blocks of highest level.

First, let's tackle the *include* relationship: a relationship from a base use case to an inclusion use case, specifying how the behaviour for the base use case contains the behaviour of the inclusion use case. The behaviour is included at the location which is defined in the base use case. The base use case depends on performing the behaviour of the inclusion use case, but not on its structure.[16] We use this relationship to avoid describing the same sequence several times by factorising the shared behaviour in its own use case.

* * *

1.11   identify a part that the different use cases have in common and factorise it in a new case included in the former.

Answer 1.11

If we examine the textual description of the *Withdraw money using a Visa card* use case in detail, we notice that steps one to five of the main success scenario will also perfectly apply to all use cases of the bank customer.

Furthermore, this main success sequence is completed by the A1 (temporarily incorrect pin number), E1 (invalid card) and E2 (conclusively incorrect pin number) alternative or error sequences.

We can therefore rightfully identify a new use case included in the previous ones that we will call *Authenticate,* and which contains the sequences quoted above. This will allow us to remove all these redundant textual descriptions from the other use cases by concentrating better on their functional specificities.

In UML, this mandatory include relationship between use cases is shown by a dashed arrow with an open arrowhead from the base use case to the included use case. The arrow is labelled with the keyword <<include>>, as indicated on the following diagram.

---

16.   From the OMG document: "Unified Modeling Language: Superstructure (version 2.0)".

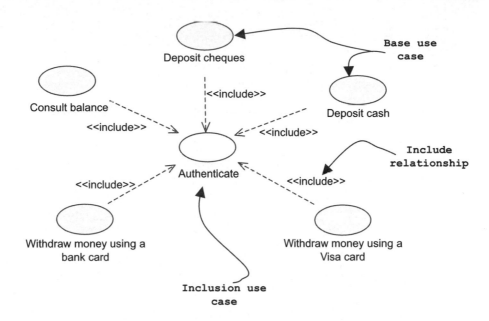

Figure 1.13 Include relationship between use cases

Note that this solution assumes that the ATM users have to re-authenticate themselves for each kind of transaction. If that is not what we require, we should instead envisage the "Authenticate" use case as a precondition for all the others, but not as an included use case.

Let's continue our analysis with the *extend*: a relationship from an extension use case to a base use case, specifying how the behaviour defined for the extension use case augments (subject to conditions specified in the extension) the behaviour defined for the base use case. The behaviour is inserted at the location defined by the extension point in the base use case. The base use case does not depend on performing the behaviour of the extension use case.[17] Note that the extension use case is optional unlike the included use case which is mandatory. We use this relationship to separate an optional or rare behaviour from the mandatory behaviour.

---

17. From the OMG document: "Unified Modeling Language: Superstructure (version 2.0)".

1.12 By extrapolating on the initial requirements, identify an extend relationship between two use cases of the bank customer.

Answer 1.12

When re-examining the withdraw money issue, it did not take us long to notice that the bank customer applies almost the same main success sequence as the Visa CardHolder. However, as a customer, he or she also has access to the other use cases: why not allow him or her to consult his or her balance just before he or she selects the desired withdrawal amount? The customer could then change the desired amount according to what is left in his or her account.

If we keep this new functional requirement, all we have to do to model it in UML is add an optional extend relationship, as demonstrated on the following figure.

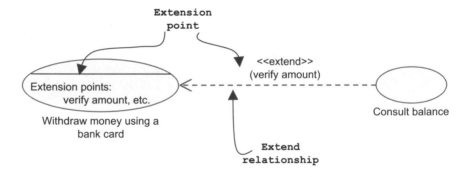

Figure 1.14 Extend relationship between use cases

The two use cases can, of course, be executed independently, but *Consult balance* can also be inserted within *Withdraw money using a bank card*, at the *Verify amount* extension point. This extension point must be declared in the textual description, for example, by modifying the nominal sequence, as we have done here:

...

7. The VISA authorisation system confirms its agreement and indicates the daily withdrawal limit.

8. The ATM asks the Bank customer to enter the desired withdrawal amount.

    Extension point: Verify amount

9. The Bank customer enters the desired withdrawal amount.

10. The ATM checks the desired amount against the daily withdrawal limit.

...

Finally, let's continue with the *generalisation* relationship: the child use cases inherit the behaviour and meaning of their shared parent use case. Nevertheless, each can include additional specific interactions, or modify the interactions that they have inherited. We use this relationship to formalise any important variations on the same use case.

*** 1.13 Identify a generalisation relationship that involves two use cases of the bank customer.

Answer 1.13

Let's consider the following two use cases: *Deposit cash* and *Deposit cheques*.

They both involve the same actors: the *Bank customer* as the primary actor and the *Bank IS* as the secondary actor. But in particular, they say the same thing: the possibility offered to a bank customer to deposit money using the ATM. Whether this transaction entails inserting the notes in a note reader, or simply depositing an envelope containing one or more cheques is not important. The result will be similar, that is to say, a credit line will be entered on the customer's account.

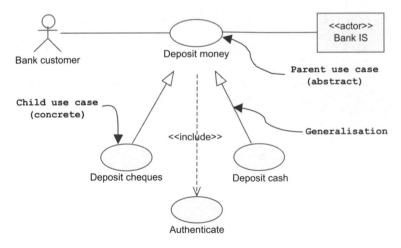

Figure 1.15 Generalisation relationship between use cases

Yet, the details of the sequences will vary considerably: for example, cash deposits require a device that will recognise the various notes, with interactions linked to each time notes are inserted, possible errors (unrecognisable note, etc.) and the end of the transaction. It is also likely that the system for the upkeep of accounts (which belongs to the *Bank IS*) is informed of the deposit in real time in order to credit the account. As for cheque deposits, though, these will involve a bank clerk carrying out a manual verification well after the transaction has finished.

In order to formalise this functional unit, whilst simultaneously retaining the possibility of describing the differences at sequence level, we use the generalisation relationship. All you have to do is add a generalised use case called *Deposit money*. This new case has the special feature of being abstract (which is shown by the *italics*), as it cannot be directly instantiated, but instead, only through one of its two specialised cases.

Notice also that the include relationship with the *Authenticate* use case is now automatically shared by the children use cases.

So, what happens to our use case diagram with all these additions? It is now so complex (compared to Figure 1.4) that it would be deceptive to think that it might be readable in a single page, as the following diagram shows.

To improve our model, we will therefore organise the use cases and reassemble them into coherent groups. To do this, we use the general-purpose mechanism for grouping elements in UML, which is called *package*.

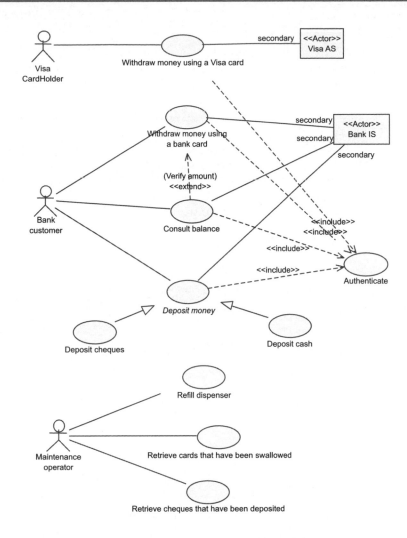

Figure 1.16 Complete use case diagram of the ATM

** 1.14 Propose structuring the use cases of the ATM into packages. Once you have done that, then develop one use case diagram for each package.

Answer 1.14

There are several possible strategies: proceed with grouping by actor, by functional domain, etc. In our example, grouping use cases by primary actor is natural, as this also allows the secondary actors to be distributed.

The inclusion use case, Authenticate, is placed in a separate package as a shared support service, in order to distinguish it from the real functional cases which include it. The dependency arrows between packages synthesise the relationship between the contained use cases. The following diagram presents the proposed structuring of the use cases by making the primary actor appear in front of each package to remind us which actor is connected to which package.[18] Note that the use of double-headed filled arrows to connect packages to their primary actors is not UML syntax, but here only to explain the packaging.

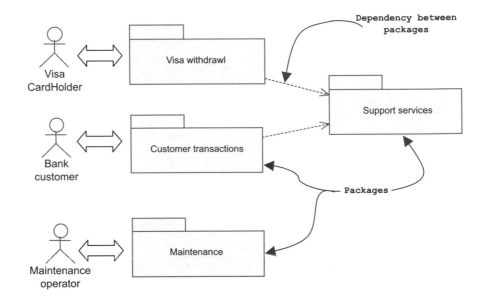

Figure 1.17   Structuring of the ATM use cases

---

18.   UML 2.0 has just added the concept of "package diagram": A diagram that depicts how model elements are organised into packages and the dependencies among them, including package imports and package extensions. Figure 1.17 belongs to this kind of organisational diagram.

We can now create a use case diagram for each of the three main packages.

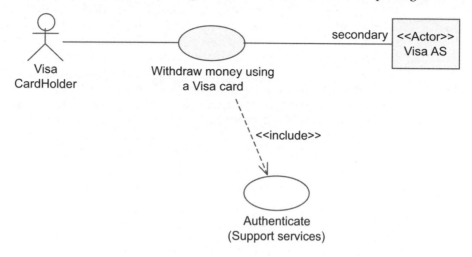

Figure 1.18   Use case diagram of the Visa withdrawal package

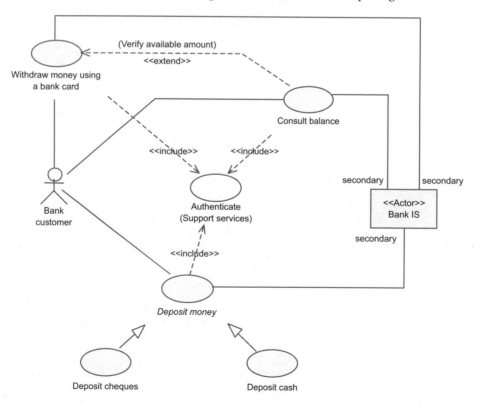

Figure 1.19   Use case diagram of the Customer transactions package

Note that Figure 1.19 is still complex, mainly because we chose to show graphically the relationship between use cases. You must be aware that these UML constructs are potentially dangerous in that the more complex syntax makes the diagram less intuitively obvious to read. They can also lead to modelling errors, that is why many practitioners tend to discourage using them. For instance, Rosenberg[19] points out in his "Top 10 Use Case Modelling Errors": *Spend a month deciding whether to use include or extend*! And Cockburn[20] explicitly warns: "if you spend much time studying and worrying about the graphics and the relations, you are expending energy in the wrong place. Put it instead into writing easy-to-read prose."

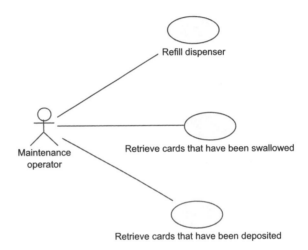

Figure 1.20   Use case diagram of the Maintenance package

Bibliography

[Adolph 02]   *Patterns for Effective Use Cases*, S. Adolph, P. Bramble, Addison-
                     Wesley, 2002.

[Bittner 02]   *Use Case Modeling*, K. Bittner, I. Spence, Addison-Wesley, 2002

[Booch 99]   *The Unified Modeling Language User Guide*, G. Booch, Addison-
                     Wesley, 1999.

---

19. *Applying Use Case Driven Object Modeling with UML: An Annotated e-Commerce Example*,
     D. Rosenberg, K. Scott, Addison-Wesley, 2001.

20. *Writing Effective Use Cases*, A. Cockburn, Addison-Wesley, 2001.

[Cockburn 01]   *Writing Effective Use Cases*, A. Cockburn, Addison-Wesley, 2001.

[Fowler 03]   *UML Distilled* (3rd Edition), M. Fowler, K. Scott, Addison Wesley, 2003.

[Jacobson 99]   *The Unified Software Development Process*, I. Jacobson et al., Addison Wesley, 1999.

[Kulak 03]   *Use Cases: Requirements in Context* (2nd Edition), D. Kulak, E. Guiney, Addison-Wesley, 2003.

[Larman 01]   *Applying UML and Patterns, (2nd Edition): An Introduction to Object-Oriented Analysis and Design*, C. Larman, Prentice Hall, 2001.

[Rosenberg 99]   *Use Case Driven Object Modeling with UML*, D. Rosenberg, Addison-Wesley, 1999.

[Rosenberg 01]   *Applying Use Case Driven Object Modeling with UML: An Annotated e-Commerce Example*, D. Rosenberg, K. Scott, Addison-Wesley, 2001.

[Rumbaugh 99]   *The Unified Modeling Language Reference Manual*, J. Rumbaugh, Addison-Wesley, 1999.

[Schneider 01]   *Applying Use Cases: A Practical Guide* (2nd Edition), G. Schneider, J. Winters, Addison-Wesley, 2001.

Complementary exercises

Aims of the chapter

In this chapter, two new case studies will allow us to complete our study of the main difficulties, which concern the implementation of the use case technique.

For the first case study, we will elaborate a complex use case diagram (with relationship between use cases), and add an advanced notation: navigability on associations between actors and use cases. Then we will introduce the difference between essential use case and real use case, a concept that was initially put forward by C. Larman,[21] and see how it influences the textual description of use cases. An example of a state diagram showing the forced sequence of system operations (another interesting concept from Larman) will follow.

The second case study gives an example of how to use the UML concepts of actors and use cases to model the business of a company, and not only an information system. We will introduce business modelling stereotypes such as business worker and business actor and see how to utilise them in use case diagrams. Then we will illustrate the important activity diagram, proposed by UML to describe business processes. To end this case study we will see how business modelling can help to find actors and use cases for a future software system.

Case study 2A – Problem statement

This exercise concerns a simplified system of a supermarket cash register. It is inspired to a great extent by the case study of C. Larman's first book (the Point-of-Sale System), which formed the basis of the Valtech training about OOAD.[22]

---

21. Refer to *Applying UML and Patterns* (2nd Edition), Prentice-Hall, 2001.

22. Object Oriented Analysis and Design.

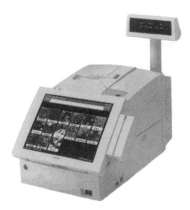

The standard procedure of using a cash register is as follows:

- A customer arrives at the checkout to pay for various items

- The cashier records the bar code number of each item, as well as the quantity if it is greater than one.

- The cash register displays the price of each item and its description.

- When all the purchases are recorded, the cashier indicates the end of the sale.

- The cash register displays the total cost of the purchases.

- The customer selects his or her payment method:

  - Cash: the cashier takes the money from the customer and puts it in the cash register, the cash register indicates how much change the customer is to be given;

  - Cheque: the cashier verifies that the customer is financially solvent by sending a request to an authorisation centre via the cash register;

  - Credit card: a banking terminal forms part of the cash register. It sends a request for authorisation to an authorisation centre, according to the card type.

- The cash register records the sale and prints a receipt.

- The cashier gives the receipt to the customer.

Once the items have been entered, the customer can present money off vouchers for certain items to the cashier. When the payment transaction is finished, the cash register sends the information on the number of items sold to the stock management system.

Every morning, the shop manager initialises the cash registers for the day.

*** 2.1 Construct a detailed use case diagram of the cash register.

Do not hesitate to use relationships between use cases in order to make your diagram more precise.

Answer 2.1

First, a simplistic solution entails identifying a "big" use case, which contains the entire standard procedure involved in using the cash register, and another use case that deals with initialisation of the cash register by the shop manager.

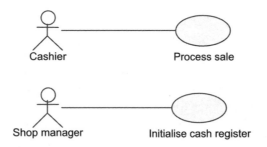

Figure 2.1   First draft of the use case diagram

If we add the secondary actors to the previous diagram, we notice that the *Process sale* use case communicates with a large number of different actors.

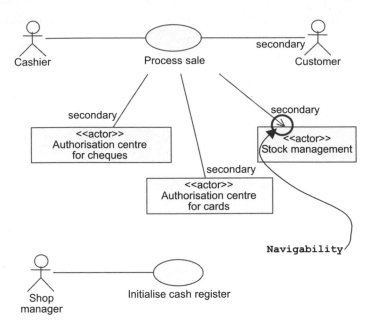

Figure 2.2 Second draft of the use case diagram

Receive-only actor

Note the use of the navigation arrow on the association with the non-human *Stock management* actor, which makes it clear that the actor can only receive messages from the system without actually sending it any in return.

This increase in the number of secondary actors leads us to deduce that this use case has too many responsibilities, and that it would therefore be sensible to divide it up into more atomic sections.

We might think that all we have to do is divide it up sequentially, as illustrated on the following figure.

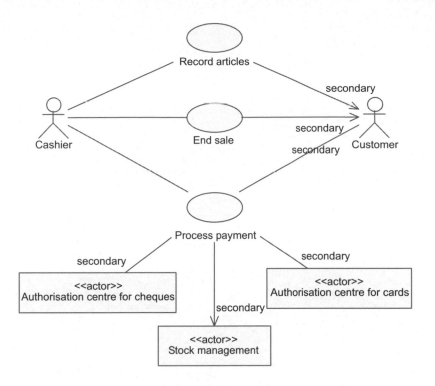

Figure 2.3 Sequential division of the main use case

Though tempting, this solution is rarely recommended. This is because the use cases that result from it no longer truly conform to the UML definition. For example, can we consider that *End sale* may represent a service that is offered by the system from start to finish?

Rather, the level of detail that is thus obtained is similar to what Larman calls *system operations*, or a unit of processing that is realised by the system within the framework of a use case, and which can possibly be reused within another.

Recording the items and closing the sale both involve the same actors and inevitably follow one another at some point in time: there is therefore no reason to separate them. On the other hand, the important variable part, which is linked to the payment method that the customer chooses, leads to separation of the generic payment procedure – thanks to an include relationship, – from the process of dealing with cash register transactions. In this way, this enables specialised use cases to be described, with each one making specific actors appear. The first part of the problem statement can therefore be modelled as represented on the following figure.

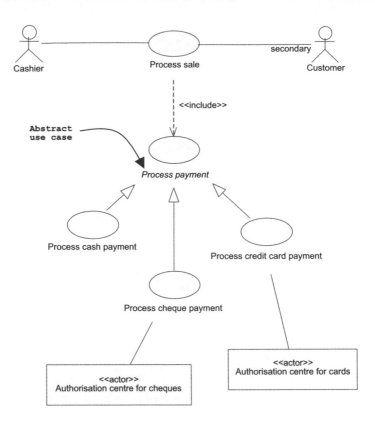

Figure 2.4   Partial use case diagram

The inclusion use case, *Process payment*, is entered in italics on the diagram to indicate that it is an abstract use case (non-instantiable). To avoid overloading the diagram, we have left out the associations with *Cashier assistant* and *Customer* on *Process payment*. However, we will note that two specialised use cases possess a specific association with an additional actor: the authorisation centre concerning them.

We can now complete the model by integrating the end of the exposition.

The optional consideration of discount coupons is conveyed quite naturally by an extend relationship with the main use case. The link with the external stock management system gives rise to a unidirectional association with a new actor. Initialisation of the cash register does not pose any difficulty. The completed use case diagram is shown below.

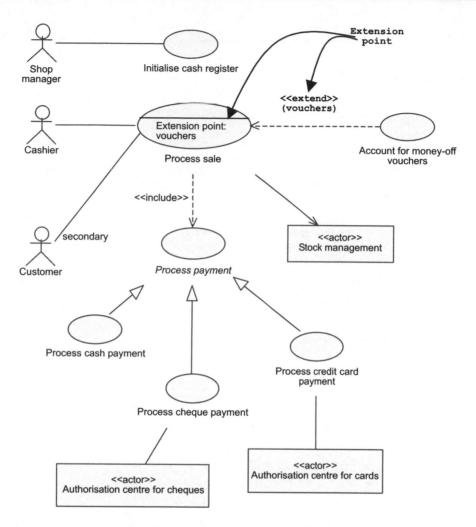

Figure 2.5 Completed use case diagram

Essential/real use case

In his previously mentioned book, C. Larman introduced the distinction between essential use case and real use case:

ESSENTIAL	REAL
Describes a process from an analysis view	Describes a process from the design view
Explains a process (relatively) independently from the hardware/ software environment	Explains a solution in terms of user interface enviroment, data input, etc.

We will illustrate this difference with the following two questions.

** 2.2   Write an essential detailed description of the main use case: *Process sale.*

Answer 2.2

Identification summary

Title: Process sale   **Type**: detailed essential

Summary: a customer arrives at the checkout with the items he or she would like to purchase. The cashier records the items and collects payment. At the end of the transaction, the customer leaves with the items.

Actors: Cashier (primary), *Customer (secondary)*.

Creation date: 05/17/02   **Date of update**: 11/10/02

Version: 1.1   **Person in charge**: Pascal Roques

Flow of events

Preconditions:

- The cash register is open; a checkout assistant is signed on to it.

Main success scenario:

1. This use case starts when a customer arrives at the checkout with items that he or she would like to purchase.

2. The cashier records each item. If there is more than one of the same item, the cashier also indicates the quantity.

3. The cash register establishes the price of the item and adds the information on the item to the sale in progress. The cash register displays the description and the price of the item in question.

4. Once the cashier has recorded all the items, he or she indicates that the sale is finished.

5. The cash register calculates and displays the total amount of the sale.

6. The cashier informs the customer of the total amount.

7. The customer chooses a payment method:
   a. In the case of cash payment, execute the "Process cash payment" use case;
   b. In the case of credit card payment, execute the "Process credit card payment" use case;
   c. In the case of cheque payment, execute the "Process cheque payment" use case.

8. The cash register records the sale that has been carried out and prints a receipt.

9. The cashier gives the cash register receipt to the customer.

10. The customer leaves with the items he or she has purchased.

"Alternative" sequences:

A1: unknown bar code number

The A1 sequence starts at point 2 of the main success scenario.

3. The cash register informs the cashier that the bar code number is unknown. The item can therefore not be included in the sale in progress.

The scenario goes back to point 2.

Error sequences:

E1: customer is unable to pay

The E1 sequence starts at point 6 of the main success scenario.

7. The customer is unable to pay the total cost with any authorised method of payment.

8. The cashier cancels the whole sale and the use case fails.

It is also necessary to describe each of the specialised use cases. We will only give a solution for the first specialised use case:

Identification summary

Title: Process cash payment

Summary: a customer pays the total displayed by the cash register in cash.

Actors: Cashier (primary), *Customer (secondary)*.

Creation date: 05/17/02   **Date of update**: 12/06/02

Version: 1.1   **Person in charge**: Pascal Roques

Flow of events

Preconditions:

*   The sale is finished.

*   The total of all items to be purchased has been displayed.

Main success scenario:

1. This use case begins when a customer chooses to pay in cash after having been informed of the total amount of the sale.

2. The customer hands over a cash amount by way of payment; it is possibly higher than the total amount of the sale.

3. The cashier registers the amount given by the customer.

4. The cash register displays the amount that has to be given back to the customer.

5. The cashier puts the money from the customer in the cash register and takes out the change owed to him or her.

6. The cashier gives the change to the customer.

"Alternative" or error sequences:

E1: customer is unable to pay

The E1 sequence starts at point 1 of the main success scenario.

2. The customer does not have enough cash to pay for the items.

3. The cashier cancels the whole sale and the use case fails, or the customer pays using another payment method (Cf. "Process cheque payment", or "Process credit card payment").

E2: cashier is unable to give change

The E1 sequence starts at point 4 of the main success scenario.

5. The cash register drawer does not contain enough change in order to give the customer the money he or she is owed.

6. The cashier asks his or her supervisor for more change, or suggests to the customer that he or she pay using a different payment method (Cf. "Process cheque payment", or "Process credit card payment").

** 2.3 Write a real detailed description of the main use case: *Process sale*.

Firstly, propose a simple dialogue window for the human-computer interface of the cashier.

Answer 2.3

The identification summary is similar to the previous one, but the type becomes: detailed real.

The proposed graphical user interface is as follows:

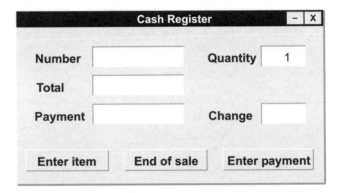

The description of the main success scenario then becomes:

1. This use case begins when a customer arrives at the checkout with items that he or she wishes to purchase.

2. The cashier records the bar code number of the product in the "Bar code number" field of the cash register's dialogue window. If there is more than one of the same item, the cashier can enter the quantity in the "Quantity" field, which has the default setting of "1". Next, the cashier presses the validation button: "Enter item".

3. The cash register establishes the price of the item and adds the information on the item to the sale in progress. The cash register displays the description (in 6 letters) and the price of the item in question in the "Total" field.

4. Once the cashier has recorded all the items, he or she presses the "End of sale" button.

5. The cash register calculates and displays the total amount of the sale in the "Total" field.

6. The cashier informs the customer of the total amount.

7. The customer chooses a payment method:

   a. In the case of cash payment, execute the "Process cash payment" use case;

   b. In the case of credit card payment, execute the "Process credit card payment" use case;

   c. In the case of cheque payment, execute the "Process cheque payment" use case.

8. The cash register records the sale that has just been carried out and prints a receipt.

9. The cashier gives the till receipt to the customer.

10. The customer leaves with the items that he or she has just purchased.

To finish off, you can find the real version of *Process cash payment* below.

Main success scenario:

1. This use case begins when a customer chooses to pay in cash after having been informed of the total amount of the sale.

2. The customer hands over a cash amount by way of payment; it is possibly higher than the total amount of the sale.

3. The cashier registers the amount given by the customer in the "Payment" field. He or she then validates this by pressing the "Enter payment" button.

4. The cash register displays the amount that has to be given back to the customer in the "Change" field.

5. The cashier puts the money from the customer in the cash register and takes out the change owed to him or her.

6. The cashier gives the change to the customer.

*   2.4   Realise a system sequence diagram that describes the main success scenario of the essential use case, *Process sale*, taking only cash payment into account.

Answer 2.4

In the form of a sequence diagram, all you have to do is copy out the interactions quoted in the textual scenario of answer 2.2 by using the graphical conventions that were adopted previously:

- the primary actor, *Cashier*, on the left,

- an object representing the Cash register in the middle,

- the secondary actor, *Customer*, on the right of Cash register.

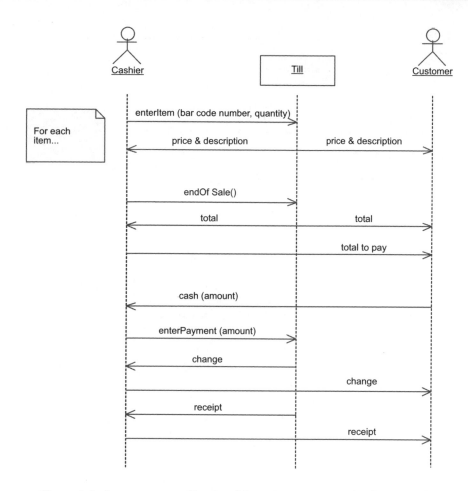

Figure 2.6 *System sequence diagram of the main success scenario* of *Process sale*

We want to add two comments to Figure 2.6:

- we have chosen to show messages being passed between actors. This is not strictly necessary, as it is outside the scope of the system, but can be envisaged if it helps the reader to validate the diagram. It represents more the business process than the system use case, but is also more significant for the domain expert.

- as the price and description are simultaneously sent to two actors, we drew the two arrows at the same horizontal level. We preferred not to use the new, but complex, *InteractionOperators* proposed by UML 2.0, such as the "weak sequencing (*seq*)".

2.5   By means of a state diagram, show the compulsory sequence of system operations for the *Process sale* use case, and continue to take only cash payment into account.

Answer 2.5

The system operations, that have been identified thanks to the previous exercise correspond to the three messages received by the system. We represent them as operations of a class stereotyped <<system>>.

<<system>> CashRegister
enterItem(bar code number, quantity) endOfSale() enterPayment(amount)

Figure 2.7 System operations of "Process sale"

In order to represent the compulsory sequence of these three system operations, with the possible repetition of the enter item procedure, a state diagram is essential. It actually represents the subset of cash register states inferred by the *Process sale* use case. Additional states are, for example, linked to the initialisation of the cash register, the connection of the cashier, etc.

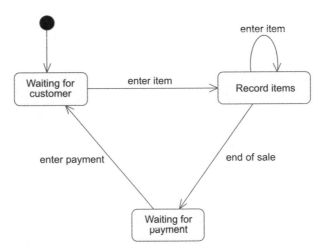

Figure 2.8 State diagram of the system operations of "Process sale"

Case study 2B – Problem statement

This second case study will give us the occasion to perform some business modelling with UML. It should be clear that the concepts that we will introduce are not part of the core UML, but are defined by an official extension to UML which is described on the OMG's Web site www.omg.org. Many modelling tools propose them, so a lot of people are currently using these graphical representations.[23]

Let's suppose that an organisation wants to improve its information system and, first of all, wishes to model the training process of its employees so that some of their tasks may be computerised.

1. The training process is initialised when the training manager receives a training request on behalf of an employee. This request is acknowledged by the person in charge who qualifies it and then forwards his or her agreement or disagreement to the person who is interested.

2. In the case of agreement, the person in charge looks in the catalogue of registered courses for a training course, which corresponds to the request. He or she informs the employee of the course content and suggests a list of subsequent sessions to him or her. When the employee has reached a decision, the training manager enrols the entrant in the session with the relevant training body.

3. If something crops up, the employee must inform the training manager as soon as possible in order to cancel the enrolment or application.

4. At the end of the employee's training, he or she must submit an assessment to the training manager on the training course that he or she completed, as well as a document proving his or her attendance.

5. The training manager then checks the invoice that the training body has sent him or her before forwarding it to the bookkeeper of purchases.

2.1 Step 1 – Business modelling

We will begin by modelling the business and processes of the organisation. This analysis will allow us to establish more easily the specifications of the information system that will support these processes.

---

23. You can find interesting articles on the subject on www.therationaledge.com.

Stereotypes for business modelling

As regards business modelling, Jacobson[24] was the first to suggest using the UML concepts of actor, use case, class, package, etc. with particular stereotypes. In the rest of the exercise, we will use the following stereotypes (which correspond to those of the RUP[25] and which are standardised by OMG in the "Business Modeling" profile):

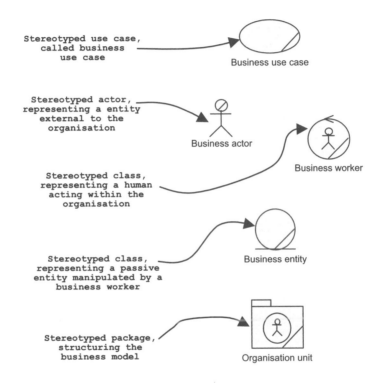

Figure 2.9 Stereotypes used for business modelling

---

24. *Software Reuse*: I. Jacobson et al., 1997, Prentice Hall, then The Unified Software Development Process, I. Jacobson, G. Booch, J. Rumbaugh, Addison-Wesley, 1999.

25. *The Rational Unified Process: An Introduction*, P. Kruchten, Addison-Wesley, 1999.

*   2.6   Draw a use case diagram that shows the training process and its actors.

Use the preceding stereotypes.

Answer 2.6

The training process is represented by a stereotyped use case.
   The actors required are (in order of the exposition):

*   the employee,

*   the training manager,

*   the training body,

*   bookkeeper of purchases.

The training body is the only entity external to the organisation, which results in the following diagram:

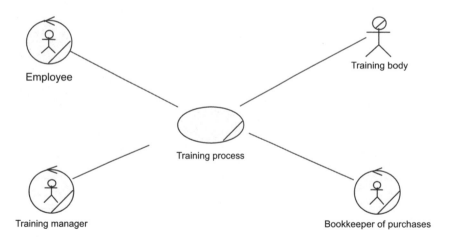

Figure 2.10 Modelling of the training process with its actors

***   2.7   Describe the dynamics of the training process by means of an activity diagram.
Use the columns (or *swimlanes*) to assign responsibilities to the actors.

Answer 2.7

The training process comprises a set of activities, which have already been organised and assigned to one of the actors identified previously. This sequence is represented perfectly using an activity diagram.

"Swimlanes" enable the activities to be arranged graphically in such a way that those that are assigned to the same actor can be found in the same vertical strip.

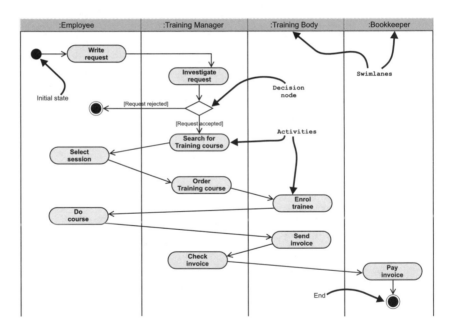

Figure 2.11   Activity diagram of the training process

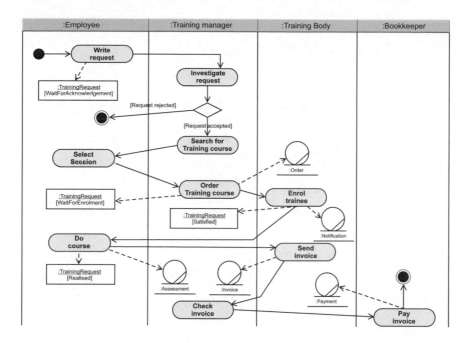

Figure 2.12   Completed activity diagram of the training process

In order to complete the first diagram, we have added the creation and change in state of the business entities following the realisation of the activities.

Note that we did not use the specific icon of the business entity for the *TrainingRequest* entity in order to be able to indicate its state inside the box.

The resulting diagram is very interesting as it acts as a bridge between the three modelling axes: functional (activities), dynamic (transitions) and static (object flows and swimlanes)!

2.2 Step 2 – Defining system requirements

Let's continue with our functional study. The definition of tasks that will be computerised is achieved by selecting certain activities of the business model. We will thus deduce the functional specifications of the information system from the preceding study, and in particular, from the activity diagram.

The system must allow a training request to be initialised and this request to be followed right up to the effective enrolment of an employee.

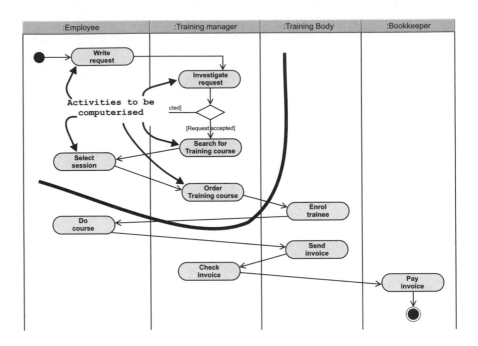

Figure 2.13   Activities of the training process, which are to be computerised

One benefit of this technique is that it clearly shows what is outside the scope of the software system: we do not need to interview the bookkeeper or handle invoices.

The system for managing training requests must therefore allow the following business activities to be automated:

- Write a request (employee),

- Investigate a request (training manager),

- Look for a training course (training manager),

- Select a session (employee),

- Order a training course (training manager).

Furthermore, we must not forget that an employee is able to cancel an application or enrolment in a session.

For all these processes, it is essential that the information system manages a registered training catalogue, to which employees can have partial access by reading what is available, and the training manager total access by having the authority to amend courses. This catalogue will not only contain the technical content, length of course, etc., of training courses offered by the registered bodies, etc., but also the dates and locations of the subsequent sessions. The training manager will also be able to organise training courses according to subject.

** 2.8 Develop the use case diagram of the information system for managing training requests.

Write a few lines by way of a summary for each use case.

Answer 2.8

According to the list of business activities, we can define the following use cases:

• Apply for training:

The employee can consult the catalogue and select a theme or course, or even a particular session. The application is automatically registered by the system and forwarded by e-mail to the training manager. If the employee has not chosen a session, but simply a course or a theme, the training manager will consult the catalogue and select the sessions that appear to correspond most to the application. This selection will be forwarded by e-mail to the employee, who will then be able to submit a new, more specific application.

• Order a training course:

Once an employee has applied for training, and this is accepted, the training manager will use the system to send – automatically by fax – an enrolment application in the form of an order form to the body involved.

• Cancel an application:

The employee may consult the current status of his or her training requests and cancel them personally. The training manager is automatically notified by e-mail.

• Maintain catalogue:

The training manager can enter a new course in the catalogue, modify an existing course or take out one that a training body has withdrawn. He or she can also modify groups of courses, which have been arranged according to theme. In addition, he or she can update the dates and locations of the sessions.

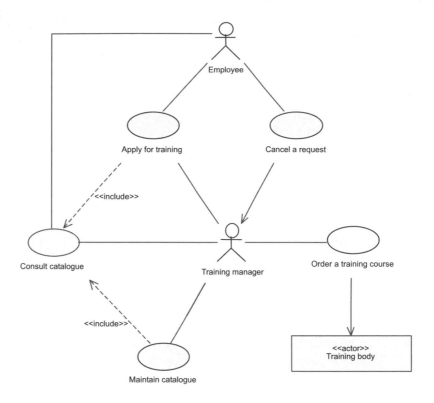

Figure 2.14 Use case diagram of the system for managing training requests

In order to be able to apply for training and maintain the catalogue, the system must offer a basic functionality for consulting the catalogue. This functionality can therefore be factorised in a new inclusion use case.

Finally, so that we do not overload the model, we will not represent the less important process of authenticating the employee or the training manager in the software system.

Figure 2.14 synthesises all these considerations.

** 2.9   Write an essential detailed description of the *maintain catalogue* use case.

Answer 2.9

Identification summary

Title: Maintain catalogue   **Type**: detailed essential

Summary: the training manager is responsible for continually updating a catalogue that lists the registered training courses available for employees. The majority of changes are from the training bodies.

Actors: person in charge of training.

Creation date: 09/28/02   **Date of update**: 08/20/03

Version: 3.0   **Person in charge**: Pascal Roques

Flow of events

Preconditions:

- The training manager has logged into the system.

Main success scenario:

1. In general, this use case starts when a training body informs the training manager of changes regarding its offer.

2. The training manager can enter a new course in the catalogue, modify an existing course or take out one that has been withdrawn by the body.

   When creating or modifying a training course, the training manager can alter the diary of sessions planned for it.

3. The system warns users that are connected to the Internet that they could well be working on an obsolete version.

   When removing a training course from the catalogue, the system shows the training manager the list of entrants who were enrolled in the cancelled sessions, and the enrolments are then cancelled.

4. If necessary, a new subject for organising courses into groups can be created.

5. The training manager validates his or her modifications.

6. The system informs the employees that are connected to the intranet that a new version of the catalogue is available.

Alternative sequences:

A1: incomplete information

The A1 sequence starts at point 2 of the main success scenario.

2. When the information relating to a new training course is incomplete (for example, absence of session dates), the training course is entered in the catalogue but enrolment on it cannot take place. The description must be modified and completed at a later stage.

The scenario continues at point 2.

Constraints:

Concurrency: this use case can only be executed by one manager at a time.

Availability: the catalogue can be accessed *via* the intranet from 9 to 5, Monday to Friday. Maintenance operations must be limited to a strict minimum during these hours.

The constraint of concurrency on this use case leads to one last question.

*   2.10 Develop the static context diagram of the system for managing training requests.

Answer 2.10

The system for managing training requests is fundamentally a multi-user one (typically an intranet), except for the training manager who must be the sole manager at a given time.

The training bodies do not have access to the system: they can only receive orders (one at a time), which explains the navigation arrow on the association between the system and the non-human actor.

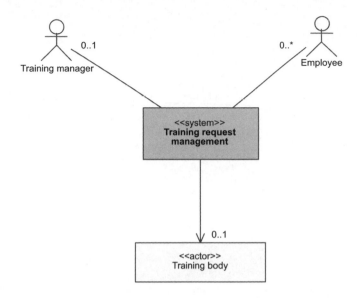

Figure 2.15 Static context diagram of the system for managing training applications

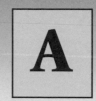

Glossary & tips

This appendix comprises a thematic glossary of the functional view (mainly inspired by the one found in the UML 2.0 Specifications from OMG), as well as a summary of tips, which have been taken from the two previous chapters.

Glossary

Action state	An action state models the realisation of a simple step, which can be neither broken down nor interrupted.
Activity state	An activity state models the realisation of a complex step that is able to be broken down into activities or actions, and which can be interrupted by an event.
Actor	Construct that is employed in use cases that define a role that a user or any other system plays when interacting with the system under consideration. Actors may represent human users, external hardware, or other subjects.
Association	Relationship between classifiers (classes, use cases, etc.), which describes a set of links. Used to link actors and use cases in the use case diagram.
Business actor	Stereotyped actor that represents an entity external to the organisation (within the context of business modelling).
Business entity	Stereotyped class that represents a passive entity, which is manipulated by a business worker (within the context of business modelling).
Business modelling	Modelling of the processes, resources and organisation of a business.
Business use case	Stereotyped use case which enables the representation of a business process (within the context of business modelling).

Business worker   Stereotyped class that represents a human acting within the business (within the context of business modelling).

Essential   Of an analytical use case, independent of all interfacing technology with the actors.

Extension   Relationship with the keyword <<extend>> from an extension use case to a base use case, specifying how the behaviour defined for the extension use case augments (subject to conditions specified in the extension) the behaviour defined for the base use case. The behaviour is inserted at the location defined by the extension point in the base use case.

Generalisation   Relationship between use cases where the children inherit the description of their shared parent; nevertheless, each of them can include additional specific interactions or modify the inherited interactions.

Inclusion   Relationship with the keyword <<include>> from a base use case to an inclusion use case, specifying how the behaviour for the base use case contains the behaviour of the inclusion use case. The behaviour is included at the location which is defined in the base use case.

Message   Specification of the conveyance of information from one instance to another, with the expectation that activity will ensue. Used in system sequence diagrams to represent the interaction between the actors and the system, which is shown as a black box.

Organisation unit   Stereotyped package that structures the business model (within the context of business modelling).

Package   General-purpose mechanism for organising elements in UML, which can be used, for example, to organise use cases into groups.

Postcondition   Boolean condition that resolves to true for the system at the end of executing a use case, apart from error scenarios.

Precondition   Boolean condition that must be true for the execution of a use case to begin.

Primary actor   Actor for whom the use case produces an observable result of value (in contrast with *secondary* actor).

Real   Of a use case described from the design view, in terms of user interface events, data input, etc.

Scenario	Specific sequence of actions that illustrates behaviours. A scenario may be used to illustrate an interaction or the execution of a use case instance. Concerning use cases, we make a distinction between main success, alternative and error scenarios.
Secondary actor	Actor that is only requested by the system at the time of the use case, or which obtains a secondary result from it (in contrast with *primary* actor).
Stereotype	Class the defines how an existing metaclass (or stereotype) may be extended, and enables the use of platform or domain-specific terminology or notation in addition to the ones used for the extended metaclass. Certain stereotypes are predefined in the UML, others may be user defined. Stereotypes are one of the extensibility mechanisms in UML.
System operation	Operation of the system that executes in response to a system event. A system event is an external input event generated by an actor to a system, within the context of a use case (from C. Larman).
Use case	Specification of a sequence of actions, including variants, that a system (or other entity) can perform, interacting with actors of the system.

Tips

- The actors are *a priori*:

  - the direct human users: identify all possible profiles without forgetting the administrator, the maintenance operator, etc.;

  - the other related systems that interact directly with the system under consideration, often by means of bidirectional protocols.

- Eliminate as much as possible "physical" actors for the benefit of "logical" actors: the actor is the one that benefits from the use of the system. In particular, this rule advises against the identification of technical interfaces that risk evolving in the course of the project, so that actors remain more stable over time.

- Use the graphical form of the *stick man* for human actors, but prefer the rectangle with the <<actor>> keyword for connected systems (if your favourite modelling tool enables it!).

- Only list the external entities that interact directly with the system (and not by means of other actors) as actors. Do not consider components internal to the system under study.

- Do not confuse role and physical entity. For instance, a single physical entity may play the role of several different actors and, conversely, a given actor may be played by multiple physical entities.

- Construct a *static context diagram*. For this, simply use a class diagram in which each actor is linked to a central class representing the system by an association, which allows the number of instances of actors connected to the system at a certain point to be specified.

- To improve the informative content of the use case diagram, we recommend that you adopt the following conventions:

  - by default, the role of an actor is "primary"; if this is not the case, indicate explicitly that the role is "secondary" on the association to the side of the actor;

  - as far as possible, place the primary actors to the left of use cases, and the secondary actors to the right;

  - if the actor can only receive messages from the system (or can only send them), use the symbol for indicating navigability restriction on the association between the use case and the actor.

- The most simple way to go about giving details of the dynamics of the use case entails compiling a written list of all the interactions between the actors and the system. The use case must have a clearly identifiable beginning and an end. It is also important to specify the possible variants, such as the the main success scenario and the different alternative or error sequences, whilst simultaneously trying to place the descriptions in a sequential order to improve their readability.

- Do not confuse *essential* use case (independent of all technological choice of interface with the actors) and *real* use case: the first is far more stable and can be reused more easily.

- Complete the textual description of use cases with one or more UML dynamic diagrams:

  - for the dynamics of the use case, use an *activity diagram* (or a state diagram for very interactive use cases);

- to describe the main success scenario, use a *sequence diagram*. Present it by placing the primary actor on the left, then an object that represents the system as a black box, and finally, by placing possible secondary actors requested in the course of the scenario to the right of the system.

- You can expand the system sequence diagram of the main success scenario so as to make the following appear:

  - the main internal activities of the system (by means of messages that it sends to itself),

  - references to "alternative" and error sequences (by means of notes).

- Use the include relationship between use cases in order to avoid having to describe the same flow of events several times. Do this by factorising this shared behaviour in an additional inclusion use case. Do not misuse this relationship for functional decomposition! Inclusion use cases are very often small reusable use-case fragments.

- Use the extend relationship between use cases in order to separate an optional or rare complex behaviour from mandatory behaviour. The extension use case should be completely separate from the extended base use case. The base use case should be complete by itself and not require the extension. Otherwise, you must use alternative scenarios to describe additional behaviour.

- Use the generalisation/specialisation relationship between use cases to formalise important variations on the same use case.

- Be moderate with relationships between use cases (include, extend, generalisation): they make use case diagrams difficult to decipher for the business experts who are supposed to check them.

- Limit the number of your concrete use cases to 20 (apart from inclusion/ extension fragments and generalisation considerations). With this arbitrary limit, first suggested by Ivar Jacobson himself, we avoid the common error in identifying use cases to represent individual steps, operations or transactions.

Part 2

Static view

Case study: flight booking system

Aims of the chapter

On the basis of a new case study, this chapter will allow us to outline the main difficulties, step by step, that the construction of UML class diagrams poses.

The class diagram has always been the most important diagram in all object-oriented methods. This is the diagram that automatic code generation tools use first and foremost. This is also the diagram that contains the widest range of notations and variants; hence the difficulty in using all these concepts correctly.

In this important chapter we will learn to:

- identify domain concepts and model them as classes;

- identify associations between concepts;

- think about the multiplicity on each side of an association;

- add attributes to domain classes;

- understand the difference between analysis and design levels;

- use object diagrams to illustrate class diagrams;

- use association classes, constraints and qualifiers;

- structure our model into packages;

- understand what is an analysis pattern.

Elements involved

- Class, object

- Operation

- Association, multiplicity

- Attribute, derived attribute

- Aggregation, composition

- Association class, qualifier

- Constraint, metaclass

- Package

- Generalisation, abstract class.

Case study 3 – Problem statement

This case study concerns a simplified flight booking system for a travel agency.

The interviews that we had with domain experts enabled us to summarise their knowledge of the field in the form of the following sentences:

1. Airline companies offer various flights.

2. A flight is open to booking and closed again by order of the company.

3. A customer can book one or more flights and for different passengers.

4. A booking concerns a single flight and a single passenger.

5. A booking can be cancelled or confirmed.

6. A flight has a departure airport and an arrival airport.

7. A flight has a departure day and time, and an arrival day and time.

8. A flight may involve stopovers in airports.

9. A stopover has an arrival time and a departure time.

10. Each airport serves one or more cities.

From the basis of these "bits of knowledge", we will construct a static domain model by following a series of steps.

3.1 Step 1– Modelling sentences 1 and 2

Firstly, we will model sentence 1:

1. Airline companies offer various flights.

AirlineCompany and *Flight* are important concepts of the real world; they have properties and behaviours. They are therefore candidate classes for our static modelling.

We can initiate the class diagram as follows:

Figure 3.1 Modelling of sentence 1

The "1..*" multiplicity to the side of the *Flight* class was preferred to a multiplicity of "0..*", as we are only managing airline companies that offer at least one flight.[26]

However, the sentence does not give us any indication of the multiplicity to the side of the *AirlineCompany* class. This is the first question we will have to ask the domain expert.

Subsequently, we will start from the notion that a flight is offered most often by a single airline company, but that it can also be shared among several charterers. As we work through this exercise, we will note that the term, "charterer" is a good candidate to name the role played by the *AirlineCompany* class in the association with *Flight*.

Figure 3.2 Completed modelling of sentence 1

We will now deal with the second sentence. The notions of opening and closing the booking represent dynamic concepts. They concern changes in state of an object, *Flight*, by order of an object, *AirlineCompany*. An obvious solution therefore consists in inserting an enumerated attribute, *state*, as shown on the following figure.

---

26. Of course this is true in domain modelling. During design we will probably shift towards "0..*", as when you add a new Airline in the system, it does not propose flights at once...

Figure 3.3   First modelling of sentence 2

This is actually not the right approach: every object possesses a current state on top of the values of its attributes. This belongs to the intrinsic properties of the object concepts. The notion of state must therefore not appear directly as attribute on class diagrams: it will be modelled in the dynamic view using the state diagram (see Chapters 5 and 6). In the UML class diagram, the only available dynamic concepts are the operations.

As it happens, beginners in object-oriented modelling often have difficulty in placing operations in the right classes! More generally, the correct allocation of responsibilities to the right classes is a distinctive feature of experienced object-oriented designers...

*   3.1   In which class do you place the operations that we have just identified?

Answer 3.1

Who is open to the booking? It is the flight, not the company.

In object-oriented design, we consider that the object on which we will be able to realise a process must declare it as an operation. The other objects that will have a reference on it will then be able to send it a message, which invokes this operation.

We must therefore place the operations in the *Flight* class, and make sure that the *AirlineCompany* class actually has an association with it.

Figure 3.4   Correct modelling of sentence 2

The *offers* association will be instantiated in a set of links between objects of the *AirlineCompany* and *Flight* classes.

It will therefore allow messages of booking opening and closing to circulate between these objects, as demonstrated on the collaboration diagram below.[27]

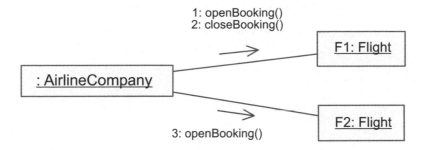

Figure 3.5 Collaboration diagram illustrating sentence 2

3.2 Step 2 – Modelling sentences 6, 7 and 10

Let's continue with the modelling of the *Flight* class. Sentences 6 and 7 refer to it directly. Let's first of all consider sentence 7:

7. A flight has a departure day and time and an arrival day and time.

All these notions of dates and times simply represent pure values. We will therefore model them as attributes and not as fully-fledged objects.

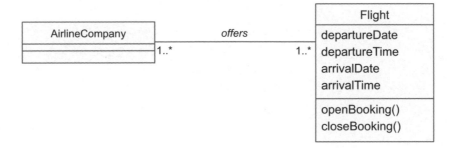

Figure 3.6 Modelling of sentences 1, 2 and 7

An object is a more "important" element than an attribute. A good criterion to apply here can be stated in the following way: if we can ask an element for its value

---

27. The collaboration diagram (renamed *communication diagram* in UML 2.0) shows how instances send messages to other instances. For a message to be received, an operation with the same name must exist in the corresponding class.

only, it concerns a simple attribute; if several questions apply to it, though, an object that possesses several attributes itself is involved, as well as links with other objects.

Try to apply this principle to sentence 6:

6.   A flight has a departure airport and an arrival airport.

*** 3.2   What are the different solutions for modelling sentence 6, together with their advantages and disadvantages?

Answer 3.2

Unlike the notions of time and date which are "simple" types, the notion of airport is complex; it belongs to the domain. An airport does not only possess a name, it also has a capacity, it serves cities, etc. For this reason, we prefer to create an *Airport* class rather than simple attributes of *departureAirport* and *arrivalAirport* in the *Flight* class.

An initial solution consists in creating an association with a multiplicity of 2 placed to the side of the *Airport* class. But in doing so, we lose the notions of departure and arrival. A trick would be to add a constraint {ordered} to the side of *Airport*, to indicate that the two airports linked to the flight are ordered (arrival always takes place after departure!).

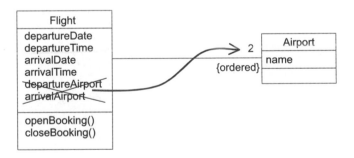

Figure 3.7   Solution that approximates to sentence 6

This entails a "warped" modelling that we do not recommend, as it is not very informative for the business expert, and in any case, a far better solution exists...

Another tempting solution would be to create two subclasses from the *Airport* class.

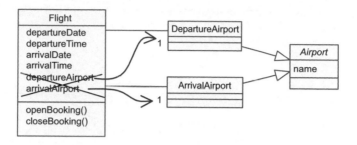

Figure 3.8   Incorrect solution of sentence 6

However, this solution is incorrect! Indeed, every airport is the departure airport for certain flights and arrival airport for others successively. The *DepartureAirport* and *ArrivalAirport* classes therefore have exactly the same redundant instances, which should discourage us from forming two distinct classes from them.

The UML concept of role works perfectly in this situation. So, the most precise way of going about this entails creating two associations between the *Flight* and *Airport* classes, with each one being assigned a different role with a multiplicity equal to 1 exactly.

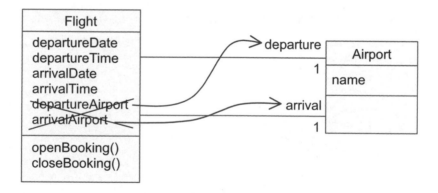

Figure 3.9   Correct modelling of sentence 6

Date as a non-primitive data type

We have already explained why we prefer to model dates and times as attributes and not as objects, unlike with airports.

A more sophisticated solution was suggested by M. Fowler[28]: it entails the creation of a specific class, Date, and then using it to specify the type of the attribute instead of adding an association.

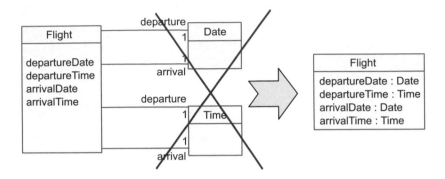

Modelling of the Date user class as a non-primitive data type

Difference between analysis model and design model

In the Java code of the final application, there is no doubt that we will explicitly use the implementation class, Date (from the `java.util` package).

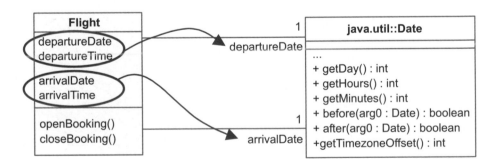

Possible fragment of detailed design class diagram aiming towards Java

It does not imply a contradiction here, but rather a difference in level of abstraction, which gives rise to two different models – an analysis model and a detailed design model – for different readers and distinct objectives.

28. *Analysis Patterns: Reusable Object Models*, M. Fowler, Addison-Wesley, 1997.

We can now deal with the modelling of sentence 10.

10. Each airport serves one or more cities.

Figure 3.10 Modelling of sentence 10

However, we notice once again that sentence 10 only concerns one direction of the association. It does not enable the multiplicity to the side of the *Airport* class to be determined. The question must therefore be formulated in the following way: By how many airports is a city served?

*   3.3   What is the multiplicity to the side of airport for the modelling of sentence 10?

Answer 3.3

The question is less trivial than it appears at first sight... Indeed, everything depends on the exact definition that is lent to the verb, "to serve" in our system! If "to serve" simply consists in naming the nearest method of air transport, then every city is served by one and only one airport.

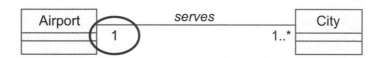

Figure 3.11 Possible modelling of sentence 10

But if "to serve" means, for example, every method of air transport, which can be found in less than thirty kilometres, then a city can be served by 0 or more airports.
  We will keep the second definition.

Figure 3.12 Completed modelling of sentence 10

3.3 Step 3 – Modelling sentences 8 and 9

Let's now consider the stopovers, i.e. sentences 8 and 9.

8.   A flight may involve stopovers in airports.

9.   A stopover has an arrival time and a departure time.

Every stopover has two properties according to sentence 9: arrival time and departure time. According to sentence 8, it is also in connection with flights and airports, which are themselves objects. It is therefore natural to make a class of it for itself.

   However, sentence 8 is also imprecise: can a stopover belong to several flights, and what are the multiplicities between *Stopover* and *Airport*? Moreover, the diagram still does not indicate the multiplicities on the *Flight* side with *Airport*.

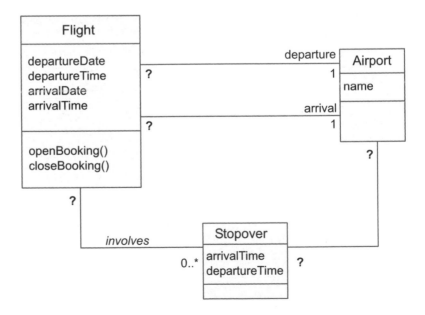

Figure 3.13 Preliminary modelling of sentences 8 and 9

** 3.4 Complete the multiplicities of the associations.

Answer 3.4

According to sentence 8, a flight can involve stopovers in airports. This wording is ambiguous, and is worth thinking about a little, maybe by resorting to the advice of a domain expert.

We can start by adding the multiplicities between *Stopover* and *Airport*, which appears to be easy. It is obvious that a stopover takes place in one and only one airport, and that an airport can be used for several stopovers. In the same way, an airport can be used as a departure or arrival airport for several flights.

We might also think that a stopover belongs to one flight and only one, but is this really certain? After consulting with the domain expert, we obtained a counter-example in the form of the following object diagram.[29]

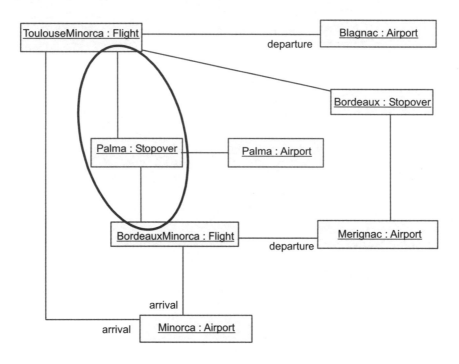

Figure 3.14 Object diagram illustrating sentence 8

29. Toulouse and Bordeaux are the main cities of the South-West of France, with Blagnac and Merignac being their airports, respectively, Palma and Minorca are touristy Spanish resorts...

A stopover can therefore belong to two different flights, particularly when these flights overlap. Note how effective it is to resort to the object diagram to give an example, or even a counter-example, which enables a tricky aspect of a class diagram to be refined.

To complete the diagram of sentences 8 and 9, all we have to do is add two pieces of information:

- the association between *Flight* and *Stopover* is an aggregation (open diamond), as it corresponds to a containment relationship. But it cannot be a composition (filled diamond), as it can be shared out;

- the stopovers are ordered with regard to flight, so we can add the standard UML coinstraint {ordered} on the side of the *Stopover* class.

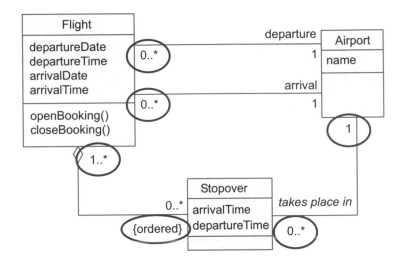

Figure 3.15 Complete modelling of sentences 8 and 9

In the previous solution, the *Stopover* class acts as a go-between for the *Flight* and *Airport* classes. It has little meaning by itself, and consequently, this makes us think of another solution concerning it...

★★★   3.5   Propose a more sophisticated solution for the modelling of stopovers.

Answer 3.5

In view of the preceding diagram, it appears that the *Stopover* class comprises little of its own information; it is strongly linked with *Airport* (multiplicity 1) and does not exist by itself, but only as part of a *Flight*.

An initial idea consists in regarding *Stopover* as a specialisation of *Airport*.

This is a very attractive solution, as the stopover automatically retrieves the name of the airport by inheritance and adds the departure and arrival times by specialisation.

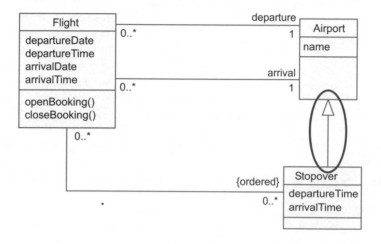

Figure 3.16 Modelling with inheritance of sentences 8 and 9

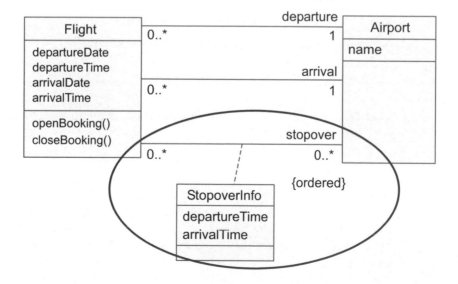

Figure 3.17 More sophisticated modelling of sentences 8 and 9

Yet, we cannot recommend that you use this solution (Figure 3.16): can we really say that a stopover is a type of airport; can we guarantee that the *Stopover* class is 100% in accordance with the specifications of its superclass? Does a stopover serve cities, can a stopover act as a point of departure or arrival for a flight? If we add the *open* and *close* operations to the *Airport* class, will they apply to *Stopover*? In actual fact, it does not concern an interface inheritance, but much rather a facility, of which an unscrupulous designer could make use in order to retrieve automatically the *name* attribute of the *Airport* class, together with its future access methods. This use of inheritance is called an implementation inheritance and furthermore, it is becoming increasingly advised against. Besides, if, one day, we want to specialise – in the business sense – airports into international and regional airports, for example, we will have to manage a multiple inheritance immediately.

Instead, why not consider this notion of stopover as a third role played by an airport with regard to a flight? The *arrivalTime* and *departureTime* attributes then become association attributes, as shown on Figure 3.17. The *Stopover* class then disappears as such, and finds itself replaced by an association class, *StopoverInfo*. We will notice the homogeneousness of the multiplicities to the side of the *Flight* class.

3.4 Step 4 – Modelling sentences 3, 4 and 5

We can now tackle the modelling process of booking.
Let's reread sentences 3 to 5, which relate to it directly.

3. A customer can book one or more flights and for different passengers.

4. A booking concerns a single flight and a single passenger.

5. A booking can be cancelled or confirmed.

A preliminary question springs to mind immediately.

* 3.6 Do we really have to make a distinction between the concepts of customer and passenger?

Answer 3.6

At first sight, this distinction can seem superfluous, but in fact, it is absolutely necessary! Let's take the case of business trips: the customer is often the employer of the person who travels for his or her job. This person then plays the role of passenger and appreciates that he or she does not need to pay the amount of his or her ticket in advance. The concept of customer is fundamental for invoicing and accounting matters, whereas the concept of passenger is more useful for aspects linked to the flight itself (boarding, etc.).

According to sentence 4, a booking concerns a single flight and a single passenger. We can model this straight away by applying two associations.

As for sentence 5, it is conveyed simply by adding two operations in the *Booking* class, following the model of sentence 2.

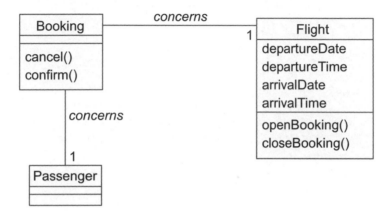

Figure 3.18 Direct modelling of sentences 4 and 5

Nevertheless, be aware that a more concise solution is possible, namely considering the passenger as a simple attribute of *Booking*. The main drawback concerns the management of information on passengers. Indeed, it is very likely that we need to manage the passenger's details (address, telephone number, e-mail address, etc.), even a frequent flyer card, which does not easily allow for the simplistic solution shown on the figure below.

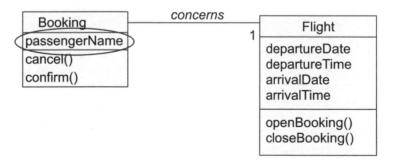

Figure 3.19 Simplistic modelling of sentences 4 and 5

We will therefore keep the first approach, which makes *Passenger* a separate class.

Let's continue with our modelling process of booking. Sentence 3 is a little more tricky because of its over-complicated wording.

** 3.7 Model sentence 3 and complete the multiplicities of the preceding associations.

Answer 3.7

The beginning of sentence 3 can be confusing due to the direct relationship that it seems to imply between customer and flight. In fact, the verb "to book" masks the concept of booking that is already identified. When modelling sentence 4, we saw that a booking concerns a single flight. The beginning of sentence 3 can therefore be re-worded more simply: a customer can make several bookings (with each one concerning a flight). This is conveyed directly by the following diagram.

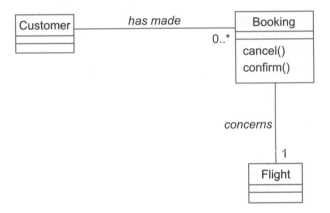

Figure 3.20 Beginning of modelling of sentence 3

We are going to complete the diagram by first of all adding the two missing multiplicities. It is clear that a booking has been made by one and only one customer, and that the same flight can be affected by zero or more bookings. Next, let's add the *Passenger* class and complete the multiplicities. How many bookings can the same passenger have? At first sight, at least one, otherwise he or she is not a passenger. We are, in fact, managing bookings, not the flight itself. We therefore need to consider persistent instances of passengers, even if they do not all have a booking at present. Once again, this is a question from a modelling standpoint! For the application that manages boarding of passengers, a passenger has one and only one booking, but here it is necessary to anticipate "0..*".

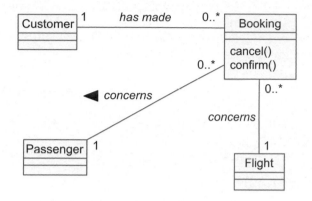

Figure 3.21 Complete modelling of sentences 4 and 5

Note the use of the direction triangle to indicate which way to read the association name.

3.5 Step 5 – Adding attributes, constraints and qualifiers

The model that we obtain through modelling the 10 sentences of the problem statement currently resembles the diagram in the figure shown below.

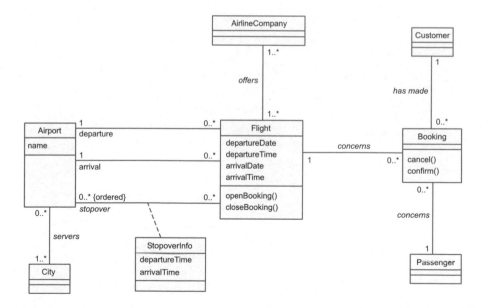

Figure 3.22 Preliminary modelling of case study 3

Some classes do not have any attribute, which is rather a bad sign for an analysis model representing domain concepts. The reason for this is simply because we have only identified the attributes that arose directly from the sentences of the problem statement. For sure, there are some missing...

*   3.8   Add the domain attributes that you consider to be essential.

Answer 3.8

For each of the classes, we will list the essential attributes below.

Be careful! We do not need to list references to other classes in the attributes: this is the very goal of identifying associations.

Airport:

- name

Customer:

- surname

- forename

- address

- telNum

- faxNum

AirlineCompany:

- name

StopoverInfo

- departureTime

- arrivalTime

Passenger:

- surname

- forename

Booking:

- date
- number

City:

- name

Flight:

- number
- departureDate
- departureTime
- arrivalDate
- arrivalTime

Note that we are using here the naming conventions that are recommended by the original developers of UML. These conventions are not mandatory but prove useful when your domain model is used afterwards at the design level.

Naming Conventions in UML

Typically, you capitalise the first letter of every word in an attribute name except the first letter (unlike the names of classes, which systematically start with an upper case letter).

The same conventions apply to the notation of association roles, as well to operations.

** 3.9 Complete the model with some relevant derived attributes.

Answer 3.9

A derived attribute is a property, which is considered interesting for the analyst, but which is redundant as its value can be computed from other elements available in the model. It is shown for clarity even though it adds no semantic information.

A good example of this is provided by the notion of *length* of a flight. It is obvious that this information is important: the customer will certainly want to know the length of his or her flight without having to calculate it him or herself! The information system must be capable of managing this notion. As it happens, the information which is necessary for this is already available in the model thanks to the existing attributes relating to the departure and arrival dates and times. This is indeed derived information. The same reasoning applies for the length of each stopover.

The diagram shown below summarises the new state of our model with all the attributes.

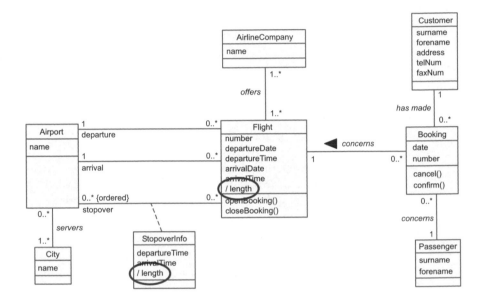

Figure 3.23   Addition of business and derived attributes

Derived attribute in design

Derived attributes allow the analyst not to make an overly premature decision with regard to design. However, as this concept does not exist in object-oriented programming languages, the designer will be led to choose between several solutions:

- Keep a plain attribute in design, which will have its access methods (*get* and *set*) as do the other attributes: you must not forget to activate the update process of the attribute as soon as an item of information is modified, on which it depends;

- Do not store the redundant value, but calculate it on request using a public method.

The second solution is desirable if the request frequency is low and the algorithm to calculate is simple. On the other hand, the first approach is necessary if the value of the derived attribute is required to be available on a permanent basis, or if the calculation is very complex and expensive. As always, the choice of the designer is a matter of compromise...

Example of conversion of a derived attribute into a design method

* * *

3.10 Refine the diagram even more by adding constraints and a qualified association.

Answer 3.10

We may well find a large number of constraints on a class diagram. It is better to make an exhaustive list of them in the text that accompanies the model, and then choose the most important ones with care, which we will then be able to insert in the diagram. Otherwise, we run the risk of overloading the diagram and making it difficult to follow.

On our example, we decided to show the strongest constraints between the attributes. They correspond to business rules that will have to be implemented in the final information system.

We have also emphasised the fact that a booking concerns a single flight and a single customer, and is irreversible into the bargain. To change flight or customer, the booking in question must be cancelled and a new one created. This can be conveyed in UML by constraints {frozen}[30] on the association roles concerned.

Finally, we have converted the *number* attribute of the *Flight* class into a qualifier of the *offers* association between the *AirlineCompany* and *Flight* classes. Indeed, each flight is identified uniquely by a number appropriate for the company. Note how

---

30. Even though {frozen} seems to have disappeared from the standard constraints with UML 2.0, you can still use this interesting convention.

the addition of the qualifier reduces the multiplicity to the side of the *Flight* class. The figure presented below shows the completed class diagram.

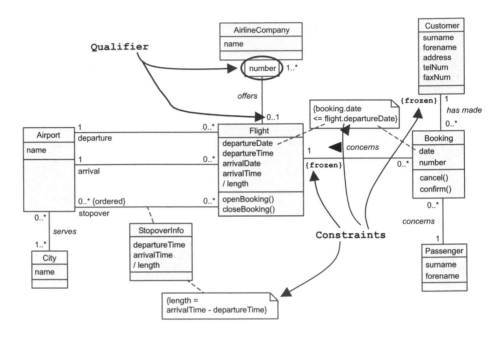

Figure 3.24 Addition of the constraints and qualifier

3.6 Step 6 – Using analysis patterns

There's room for even more improvement in our model!

To this end, let's go back to the elements that concern the *Flight* class, as represented on the following figure. Do you not think that the *Flight* class has many different responsibilities, considering all its attributes and associations? It violates a strong principle of object-oriented design, which some authors call *high cohesion*.[31]

---

31. One of the most important responsibility assignment patterns (GRASP) according to C. Larman. Refer once again to *Applying UML and Patterns* (2nd Edition), Prentice Hall, 2001.

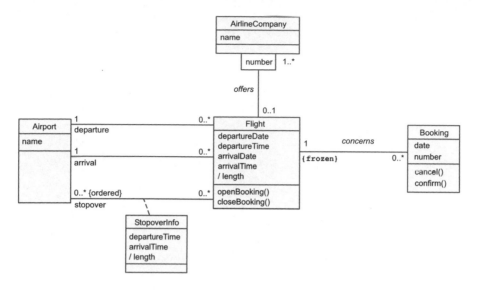

Figure 3.25 Detail of the model concerning the *Flight* class

**** 3.11 Propose a more sophisticated solution for modelling the flights.

Answer 3.11

The *Flight* class from the preceding diagram has two different types of respons-ibilities:

- The first concerns all information that can be found in the schedules of airline companies: yes, there is indeed a nonstop flight from Toulouse-Paris Orly every Monday morning at 7h10, offered by Air France... This is a generic flight, which is available every week, or near enough every week.

- The second gathers information relating to bookings. You are not booking a Toulouse-Paris Orly flight on Monday morning, but rather the Toulouse-Paris Orly flight on 25 January 2004!

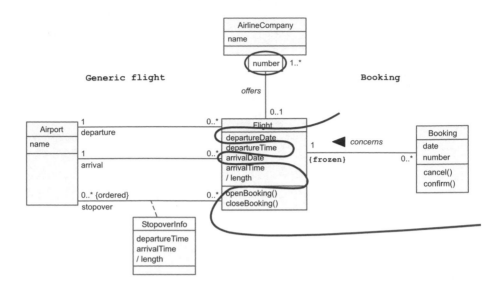

Figure 3.26   Separation of the responsibilities of the *Flight* class

Looking at the preceding figure, we can see a type of instantiation relationship between a *GenericFlight* class limited to the first type of responsibilities, and a *Flight* class that gathers the responsibilities of the second type.

Indeed, a generic flight describes once and for all properties that will be identical for numerous real flights.

Likewise, let's suppose that a company cancels all its subsequent weekend flights departing from airport X, as these are unavailable until further notice due to considerable maintenance work being carried out every Saturday and Sunday. In our first solution, this signifies that we are going to get rid of all corresponding instances of the *Flight* class. At the end of the maintenance period of airport X, we will have to recreate the instances of *Flight* with their valued attributes and their links from scratch. If we take a *GenericFlight* into account, however, the values of the attributes and the links of the flights leaving from X are not lost; there will simply not be a corresponding, real instance of *Flight* for three months.

To update the model, all you have to do is:

- distribute the attributes, operations and associations of the former *Flight* class among the two classes of *GenericFlight* and *Flight*;

- add an association, "1-*" *describes*, between *GenericFlight* and *Flight*.

Moreover, we have added two attributes in the *GenericFlight* class to indicate the weekday of the flight, and the time of year when it is available. An additional constraint links the values of the *departureDate* attributes of the *Flight* class and of the *GenericFlight* class.

validityPeriod with a non-primitive data type

The *validityPeriod* is not a simple attribute: we can ask it for its beginning, end, length, etc. A solution has been put forward by M. Fowler[32]: create a class called *TimePeriod* (as for *Date* previously), and then use it to specify the type of the attribute.

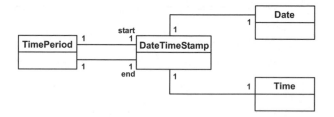

Modelling of the "non-primitive" type, TimePeriod

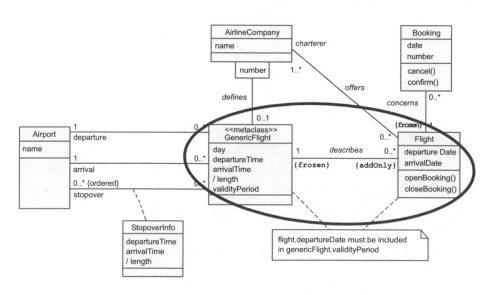

Figure 3.27 Distribution of responsibilities among GenericFlight and Flight

---

32. *Analysis Patterns: Reusable Object Models*, M. Fowler, Addison-Wesley, 1997.

Finally, we must see to it that sentence 2 is respected. A flight is open or closed to booking by order of the company. Here, we are dealing with the dated flight and not the generic flight. It is the same for a possible cancellation... We must therefore add a direct association between *Flight* and *AirlineCompany*, which would allow the interaction described in Figure 3.5, whilst retaining the qualified association between *GenericFlight* and *AirlineCompany*.

Figure 3.26 is therefore altered, as shown on Figure 3.27. Each of the two classes – *Flight* and *GenericFlight* – has found back high cohesion.

Metaclass pattern

The separation of responsibilities which was carried out previously can be generalised in the form of an "analysis pattern", which can be reused in other contexts.

We identify an *XX* class, which has too many responsibilities, some of which are not specific to each instance. We add a *TypeXX* class, we distribute the properties among the two classes and we link them by a "* - 1" association. The *TypeXX* class is described as a "metaclass", as is *GenericFlight* on the figure below, as it contains information that describes the *XX* class.

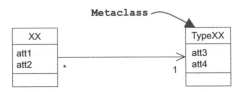

Reusable generic diagram

Note that the limited navigation from XX to TypeXX is not mandatory but is very frequent (at least in design).

3.7   Step 7 – Structuring into packages

Our domain model is now almost finished. To make using it even easier and in order to prepare the object-oriented design activity, we will structure it into packages.

Structuring into packages

Structuring a domain model is a tricky procedure. It must rely on two basic principles: *coherence* and *independence*.

The first principle entails grouping the classes that are similar from a semantic point of view. To do this, the following coherence criteria must be met:

- objective: the classes must return services of the same nature to users;

- stability: we isolate the classes that are truly stable from those that will most probably develop in the course of the project, or even subsequently. Notably, we distinguish *business* classes from *application* classes;

- lifetime of objects: this criterion enables classes to be distinguished, whose objects have very different life spans.

The second principle consists in reinforcing this initial division by endeavouring to minimise the dependencies between packages.

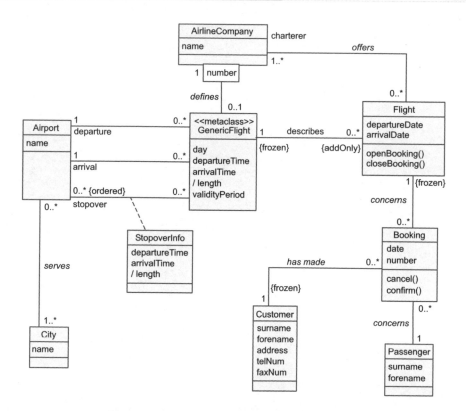

Figure 3.28 Domain model before structuring

** 3.12 Propose a division of the domain model into two packages.

Answer 3.12

According to the aforementioned criteria, we can offer an initial division into two packages:

- the first will concern the definition of flights, very stable in time, especially the section specific to *GenericFlight*;

- the second will deal with bookings, together with all their associations.

Each package contains a set of classes that are tightly linked, but the classes of the two packages are almost independent. This first division is indicated by the line that acts as a partition in the diagram shown below.

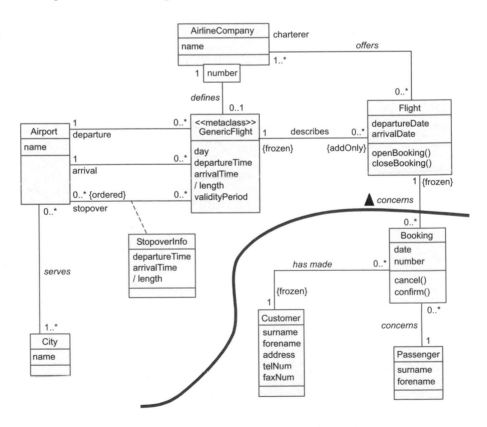

Figure 3.29 Division of the model into two independent sections

There is, however, another solution that consists in positioning the *Flight* class in the same package as the *Booking* class, as illustrated on the following diagram. The favoured criterion in this second division is the lifetime of the objects, with the instantiated flights being closer to bookings than to generic flights.

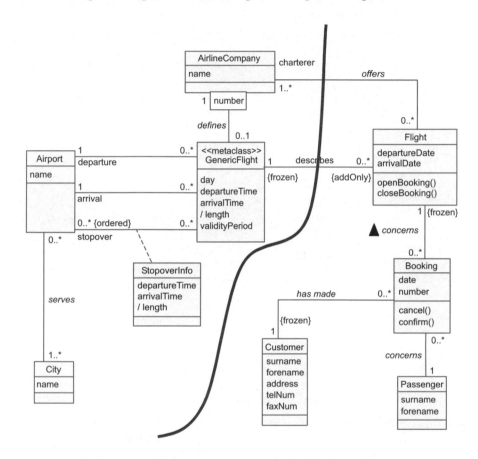

Figure 3.30 Possible second division of the model

**** 3.13 Find a solution that minimises coupling between the two packages.

Answer 3.13

In the two previous cases, we can state that at least one association traverses the boundary between the packages. The problem of associations traversing two packages resides in the fact that just one of them is enough to lead to a mutual dependency – if it is bidirectional. In fact, the object designer has to hunt down mutual or cyclical dependencies to increase the modularity and evolutionary capability of his or her application.

In the first solution, a single association is involved, as recalled in the diagram below. But this association produces a mutual dependency between the two packages all by itself.

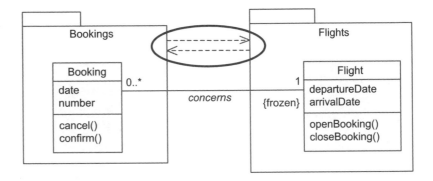

Figure 3.31 Mutual dependency between packages

Navigability and dependency

By default, an association between two classes, A and B, enables navigation in both directions between objects of class A and objects of class B.

However, it is possible to limit this navigation to only one of the two directions in order to eliminate one of the two dependencies induced by the association. UML allows us to represent this navigability explicitly by adding onto the association an arrow that indicates the only possible direction.

In our example, we will make a choice and favour a navigation direction in order to rule out one of the two dependencies. It is clear that knowledge of the flight concerned is a prerequisite of a booking, whereas a flight can exist by itself, independently of any booking.

The previous diagram can therefore be modified so that it only shows the dependency of the *Bookings* package towards the *Flights* package.

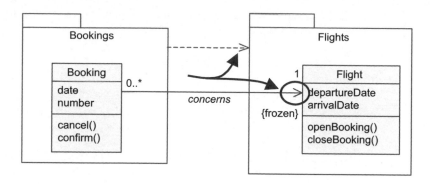

Figure 3.32 Minimised coupling between the packages

Let's now take a closer look at the second solution. This time, two associations are traversing the packages. What can we do to reduce the navigabilities of these associations?

It makes sense to fix one direction of navigability from *Flight* towards *GenericFlight*: a real flight is described by one and only one generic flight to which it must have access, whereas a generic flight can exist by itself.

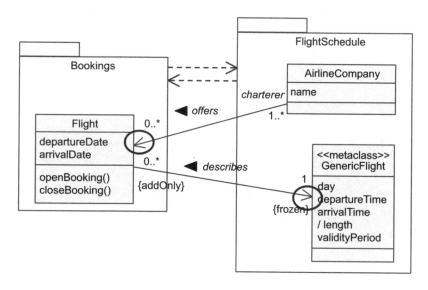

Figure 3.33 Inevitable mutual dependency for the second solution

Alas, for the second association, we already know that navigability is mandatory for *AirlineCompany* towards *Flight* due to sentence 2, and which was illustrated by the collaboration diagram in Figure 3.5.

Even if we remove the navigability of *Flight* towards *AirlineCompany*, we will end up with two navigable associations in different directions. This is enough to impose a mutual dependency between the packages, as demonstrated in Figure 3.33.

This study on the coupling of packages for the two proposed solutions therefore makes the scales tip towards the first solution, which was not at all evident from the outset.

Classes are distributed between both packages as indicated in Figure 3.34. The *Flights* package can now lend itself to re-use, unlike the *Bookings* package.

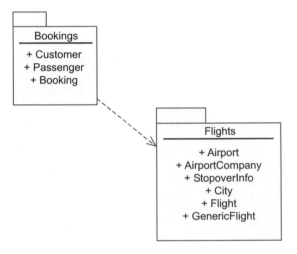

Figure 3.34   Structural diagram of packages from the solution that has been retained

The complete state of our model can now be synthesised by the following diagram.

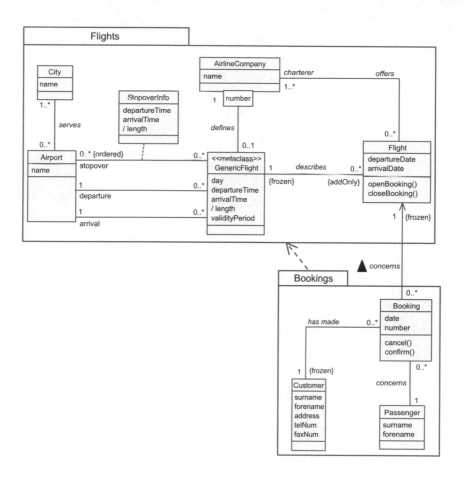

Figure 3.35 Complete model of the flight booking system

3.8   Step 8 – Generalisation and re-use

After all this work on flight bookings, we would like to expand the field of the model by offering bus trips as well – a service that carrier companies will provide.

A bus trip has a departure city and a destination city, with associated dates and times. The journey may entail stops in cities along the way.

A customer can book one or more trips and for one or more passengers.

***   3.14 By analogy with the previous figure, propose a domain model for booking bus trips.

Answer 3.14

The model is practically identical to the preceding one, including the division into packages.

It is a little simpler for two reasons:

- the notion of airport does not have an equivalent, and the *City* class is directly associated with the *JourneyByBus* class;

- the distinction between *Flight* and *GenericFlight* does not seem to be a transferable notion, as trips by bus are not as regular and, moreover, are not scheduled in advance.[33]

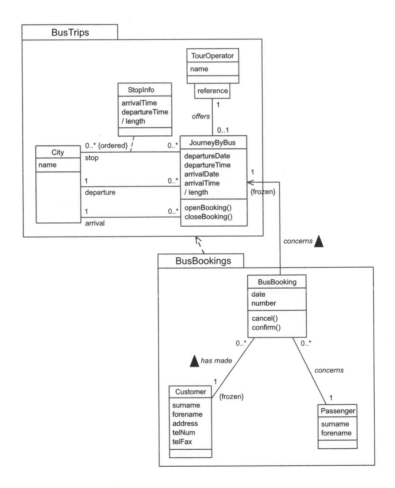

Figure 3.36 Domain model for booking bus trips

---

33. This is just an assumption! If it is relevant, we can imagine having a *Terminus* class identical to *Airport*. Then, the *BusTrips* package could well be identical to *Flights*!

It is plain to see that Figures 3.35 and 3.36 share numerous similarities:

- some classes feature in both models: *City*, *Customer*, *Passenger*;

- some classes are related to each other: *BusBooking* and *Booking*, *StopoverInfo* and *StopInfo*, etc.

We will therefore attempt to make these models merge by factorising the concepts as far as possible, in order to be able to extend their scope even further if need be (booking cruises, etc.).

* * *   3.15 Propose a merged logical architecture, which is as flexible as possible.

Answer 3.15

Two main tasks must be carried out:

- Isolation of the shared classes into new packages, so that we can re-use them;

- Factorisation of the shared properties into abstract classes.

First, let's begin by identifying and grouping together the shared classes.

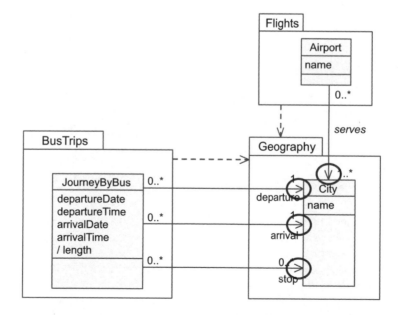

Figure 3.37 Isolation of the City class in a new re-usable package

The *City* class is very important for the description of flights and bus trips. In the model of Figure 3.36, we have actually re-used the existing *City* class, which has immediately created an unjustified dependency between the *BusTrips* and *Flights* packages. Instead of going about it this way, it would be more apt to isolate it into a separate package, which will be able to be re-used at any time; indeed, which will even be able to be bought off-the-shelf, with its instantiation per country...

So that this new package is really a re-usable component, it must not depend on application packages which contain the *Airport* and *BusTrips* classes. To this end, we have already seen that it was sufficient to act on the navigability of the associations concerned, as indicated on the diagram below.

The *Customer* and *Passenger* classes also feature in both types of bookings. It is therefore in our interest to isolate them in a new package, as was done for the *City* class. But it would not be wise to group these three shared classes together in the same package, simply because they are a feature of both model types. Indeed, the concepts that they represent bear no relation to each other...

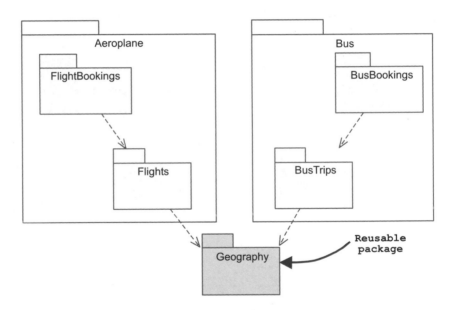

Figure 3.38 Identification of the re-usable package, Geography

After this first task of isolating the re-usable shared classes, the logical architecture is presented in the form of the above structural diagram.

We must now factorise the shared parts.

Let's begin with what is most obvious: the similarity between the *FlightBookings* and *BusBookings* packages sticks out a mile. The only difference concerns the *FlightBooking* (previously called *Booking*, and renamed for clarity) and *BusBooking* classes: they have the same attributes and operations and almost the same associations. An abstract superclass, *Booking*, is therefore essential from a logical point of view, as illustrated on the following diagram.

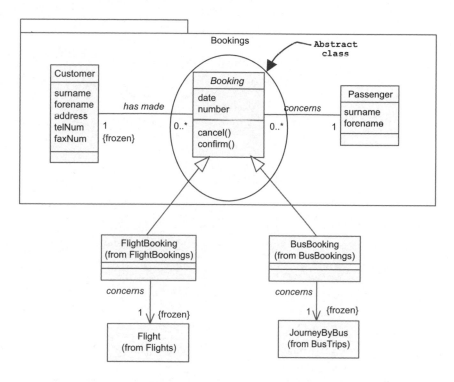

Figure 3.39 Insertion of the abstract class, *Booking* by generalisation

The abstract class, *Booking*, as well as the two classes of *Customer* and *Passenger*, which are shared by the two methods of transport, are isolated in a new package called *Bookings*. This package is called a generalised package, in comparison with the two packages of *FlightBookings* and *BusBookings*. Indeed, the two specialised packages inherit the classes of *Bookings*, and have the right to redefine some of them.

The overall diagram of the packages that are thus obtained is represented in the following figure.

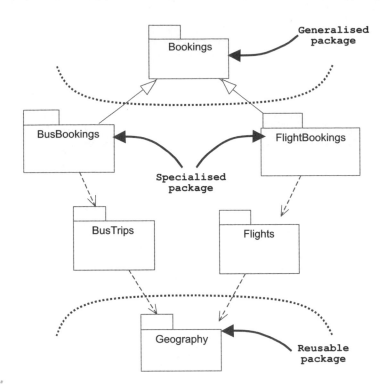

Figure 3.40   Insertion of the generalised package, *Bookings*

Bibliography

[Booch 99]   *The Unified Modeling Language User Guide,* G. Booch, Addison-Wesley, 1999.

[Coad 97]   *Object Models: Strategies, Patterns and Applications* (2nd Edition), P. Coad, D. North, M. Mayfield, Prentice Hall, 1997.

[Fowler 97]   *Analysis Patterns: Reusable Object Models,* M. Fowler, Addison-Wesley, 1997

[Fowler 03]   *UML Distilled* (3rd Edition), M. Fowler, K. Scott, Addison-Wesley, 2003.

[Gamma 95]   *Design Patterns: Elements of Reusable Object-Oriented Software,* E. Gamma et al., Addison-Wesley, 1995.

[Hay 96]   *Data Model Patterns: Conventions of Thought,* D. Hay, Dorset
                   House Publishing, 1996.

[Larman 97]   *Applying UML and Patterns: An Introduction to Object-Oriented
                   Analysis and Design,* C. Larman, Prentice Hall, 1997.

[Larman 01]   *Applying UML and Patterns: An Introduction to Object-Oriented
                   Analysis and Design* (2nd Edition), C. Larman, Prentice Hall, 2001.

[Rumbaugh 91]   *Object-Oriented Modeling and Design,* J. Rumbaugh et al., Prentice
                   Hall, 1991.

Complementary exercises

Aims of the chapter

By working through several short exercises, this chapter will allow us to complete our overview of the main difficulties involved in the construction of UML class diagrams with advanced topics such as:

- distinction between aggregation and composition;

- correct use of generalisation and abstract classes;

- correct use of association classes;

- constraints between associations (xor, subset, etc.);

- new analysis patterns such as "Party" or "Composite".

We will also push on further the business modelling of an organisation, which was introduced in Chapter 2 with the case study of the training process, from the functional view. We will now tackle it from the static view and try to discover the main business entities. This will lead us to provide a detailed illustration of the benefits gained by a lexical analysis of a text, within the context of initiating domain class diagrams. Note that we will enhance activity diagrams with object flows corresponding to the business entities further on in Chapter 6.

Structural relationships between classes

Let's study the following sentences:

1.   A directory contains files

2.   A room contains walls

3.   Modems and keyboards are input/output peripherals

4.   A stock-exchange deal is a purchase or a sale

5.   A bank account can belong to an individual or a legal entity

6.   Two people can be married.

** 4.1   Determine the appropriate static relationship (generalisation, composition, aggregation or association) for each sentence of the previous problem statement.

Draw the corresponding class diagram.

Feel free to propose various solutions for each sentence.

Answer 4.1

Sentences 1 and 2 illustrate what differentiates aggregation from composition:

1.   A directory contains files;

2.   A room contains walls.

"A directory contains files": at least one aggregation is involved here. Let's see if we can go further and form a composition from it. First criterion to verify: the multiplicity must not be higher than one on the side of the composite. This is indeed the case in the first sentence, as a file belongs to one and only one directory. Second criterion: the lifetime of the parts is to depend on that of the composite. Here again, this is the case as the destruction of a directory brings about the destruction of all the files that it contains. We can therefore consider the first sentence as an example of composition.

   Let's now carry out the same analysis on the second sentence, "A room contains walls". This time, after verifying the first criterion, we have to abandon composition, as a wall can belong to two adjoining rooms (or even more). The relationship is therefore only an aggregation one. In order to complete the multiplicities, we can consider that a room contains at least one wall (circular!).

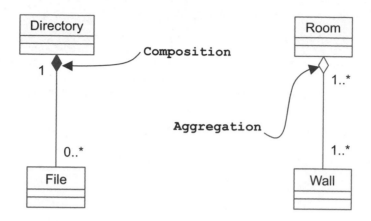

Figure 4.1 Class diagram of sentences 1 and 2

Sentences 3 and 4 are modelled in UML by generalisation relationships:

3. Modems and keyboards are input/output peripherals;

4. A stock-exchange deal is a purchase or a sale.

The only difference is the wording of sentence 4, which corresponds to a specialisation; whereas that of sentence 3 is a generalisation. However, we can add some precision to both models:

• Superclasses are abstract: they cannot be directly instantiated, but always by the means of one of their subclasses;

• The generalisation tree of sentence 3 is incomplete: there are many other input/output peripherals, such as monitors, mice, etc.

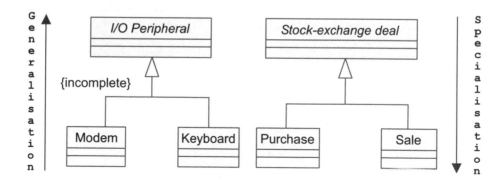

Figure 4.2 Class diagram of sentences 3 and 4

Sentence 5 is not a simple generalisation:

5. A bank account can belong to an individual or a legal entity.

Indeed, the verb phrase used is not "is a" or "is a type of", but "belongs to". It therefore concerns a simple association. An initial simplistic approach consists in describing two optional associations, as illustrated by the following figure.

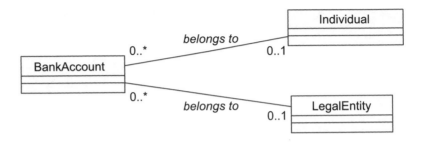

Figure 4.3 Class diagram of sentence 5 – Incorrect solution

Yet, this solution does not account for the exclusive "or" at the end of the sentence. Indeed, the preceding diagram can be instantiated just as well with a *BankAccount* object, which is simultaneously linked to an *Individual* and a *LegalEntity*, as with a *BankAccount* linked to no object. This is not what we want: a *BankAccount* object must be linked either to an *Individual*, or to a *LegalEntity*, not to both at the same time, but strictly to one of the two to the exclusion of the other.

In fact, two correct but very different solutions are possible, which consist in:

- Explicitly inserting the predefined constraint {xor} between the two associations that bear a multiplicity strictly equal to 1;

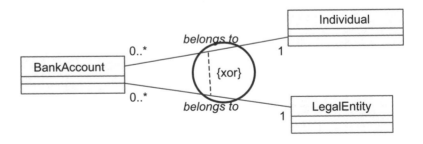

Figure 4.4 Class diagram of sentence 5 – First solution

- Inserting an abstract class by generalisation, with specialisation implicitly playing the role of "exclusive or".

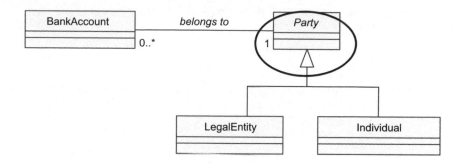

Figure 4.5 Class diagram of sentence 5 – Second solution

The two solutions are equally valid in UML and correct. This is another good example that shows that modelling is not an exact science with only one solution for a given problem. The modeller therefore has the choice between these two diagrams.

An argument in favour of the second solution is that we are probably interested in factorising attributes (*name, address,* etc.) and operations in the abstract class.

The "Party" pattern

This method of modelling entities that have a unique name and address (as do individuals or legal entities) by an abstract class and two specialised subclasses was proposed by D. Hay.[34]

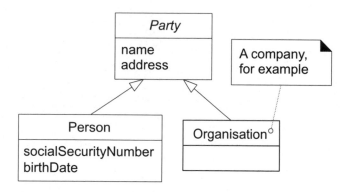

Modelling of the "Party" pattern

34. *Data Model Patterns: Conventions of Thought,* D. Hay, Dorset House Publishing, 1996.

Sentence 6 introduces the feature of defining a relationship between objects of the same class

6. Two people can be married.

This is conveyed very simply by an association between this given class and itself. The multiplicities of the diagram are deduced from the current law in most Western countries: a person is not obliged to marry, but cannot be married to several people at the same time!

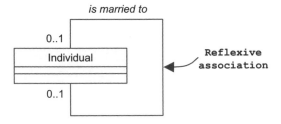

Figure 4.6 Class diagram of sentence 6

If we want to add the constraint that marriage can only unite people of the opposite sex,[35] we then have two solutions again:

* Explicitly introduce an enumerated attribute for sex: (m, f) and a constraint on the association;

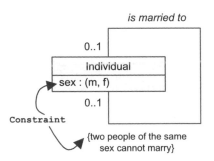

Figure 4.7 Completed class diagram of sentence 6

* Introduce two subclasses of *Male* and *Female* as demonstrated on the following figure.

---

35. Here, it depends more on the country (refer to Netherlands for example ...).

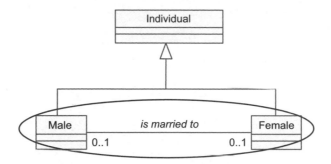

Figure 4.8 Version of the class diagram of sentence 6 with specialisation

To complete the model, let's take into account the new possibility offered by PACS ("pacte civile de solidarité", a French law on civil partnership not restricted to people of the same gender). Once again, this leads to a reflexive association – this time, it is unconstrained...

Nevertheless, we will notice that it is imperative to add a constraint that forbids people from being married to someone, and simultaneously being in a civil partnership with someone else, or in a civil partnership with oneself...

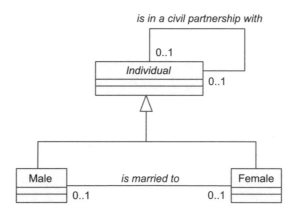

Figure 4.9 Addition of the possible relationship provided for by PACS

Moreover, the addition of the marriage date, type of contract, etc. illustrates the use of the association class. As UML does not allow an association class to have a name on the association and another one on the class, the diagram then becomes:

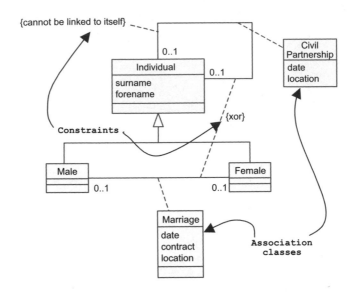

Figure 4.10 Completed version of the class diagram of sentence 6, together with association classes

** 4.2 Model the use of ballpoint pens and rollerball pens.

The problem statement is deliberately vague!

Answer 4.2

Such an imprecise problem statement is not rare at the beginning of real projects...

However, we will easily be able to construct a relevant class diagram by using our everyday knowledge of ballpoint and rollerball pens.

So, we will start by identifying two classes: *Ballpoint* and *Rollerball*, which have quite a number of shared properties (colour, brand, etc.), but which also differ from each other (for example, let's consider that ballpoint pens have a top, whereas rollerball pens only have a retractable tip). A well-informed modeller sees the possibility here of a generalisation/specialisation relationship straight away. He or she therefore inserts an abstract class to factorise the shared characteristics.

The model might already look like the following diagram:

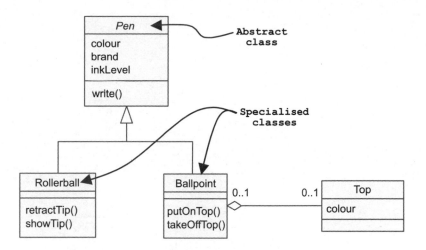

Figure 4.11 First version of the class diagram

Take note of the multiplicities between *Ballpoint* and *Top*: a ballpoint pen can lose its top, and a top the barrel of its original ballpoint pen. This notion of *Barrel* is interesting, and shared by ballpoints and rollerballs alike. To create uniformity with *Top*, we will therefore add it to our diagram.

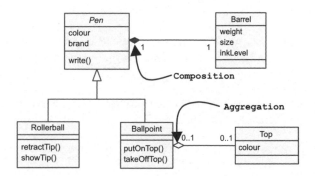

Figure 4.12 Second version of the class diagram

The relationship between *Pen* and *Barrel* is obviously one of composition. On the other hand, coherence of lifetimes does not necessarily exist between *Ballpoint* and *Top*, as my three-year-old daughter proves to me on a daily basis! Also note that the *inkLevel* attribute has been moved to the *Barrel* class. This move of an attribute from one class to the other is customary, especially in the case of composition or aggregation relationships, in order to make classes more uniform and cohesive.

To make our model even more complete, let's introduce the concept of ballpoint pen with an included eraser, and especially a class to model the user and/or the owner of the *Pen*.

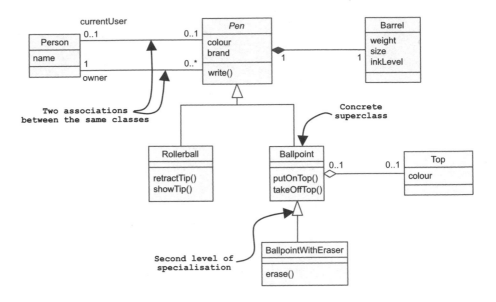

Figure 4.13 Third version of the class diagram

Notice the wise use of the two associations between the *Person* and *Pen* classes: we thereby make a precise distinction between the multiplicities that are totally different in the two cases, thanks to the names of the roles to the side of *Person*:

- A person can play the role of owner with regard to any number of *pens*, but a *pen* has one and only one owner;

- A person can use a maximum of one *pen* at any one time, and a *pen* can have a maximum of one user.

The specialisation of *Ballpoint* in *BallpointWithEraser* stands out for the following reasons:

- *Ballpoint* has not become an abstract class and possesses only one specialisation;

- The specialisation only concerns the behaviour.

We must therefore remember that a superclass is not necessarily abstract (otherwise, we would not need visual help in the form of italics as for *Pen*), and that the generalisation/specialisation relationship does not always lead to an inheritance "tree".

The constraint {frozen}

This standard constraint in UML[36] allows the addition of a detailed item of information, which may be interesting on a class diagram:

- With regard to an attribute, the fact that its value never changes during the life of an object (for example, the brand of a *Pen*);

- With regard to an association, the fact that a link between two objects can never be modified after its creation (for example, the composition link between *Pen* and *Barrel*, but not the one between *Ballpoint* and *Top*).

By default, the attributes and associations are not {frozen}.
N.B. Likewise, we could have specified that the inheritance tree of *Pen* is not complete (there are certainly types of *Pen* other than rollerballs and ballpoints) by attaching the predefined constraint, {incomplete} to it.

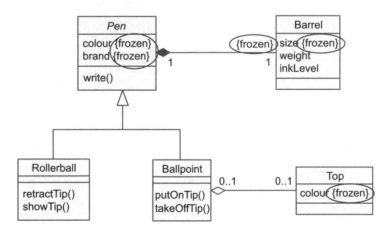

Second version of the model with the {frozen} constraints

---

36. The constraint {frozen} which existed in recent versions of UML (see for instance the description of UML 1.3 in the *UML User Guide* from G. Booch) seems to have disappeared from the standard constraints as far as concerns UML 2.0. But as we can define our own constraints, we can still use this interesting convention...

***   4.3   Propose several solutions for modelling the following sentence: "A country has a capital".

Draw corresponding class diagrams and indicate the advantages and disadvantages of the different solutions.

Answer 4.3

A sentence as simple as "A country has a capital" will enable us to illustrate the highly subjective character of the activity known as modelling, and the often difficult choice that must be made between simplicity and flexibility.

Indeed, we will propose no less than four different solutions to this question, from the most simple to the most refined...

Figure 4.14   Compact solution

First solution, the most compact one possible: a *Country* class with a simple *capital* attribute. This is sufficient if we only want to retrieve the name of the capital of each country and, for example, create a small table with two columns, with the countries ordered alphabetically...

It is difficult to make it any more simple! Subsequently, we will be able to complete the model easily by adding some attributes to the *Country* class: *name, language, currency,* etc.

On the other hand, what do we do if we want to add properties to the concept of capital, such as population, surface area, etc.? The previous solution is limited here, and we are then compelled to promote capital to the rank of class. Here, we encounter an example of the difference between class and attribute, which has already been discussed when we dealt with Question 3.2 in the preceding chapter.

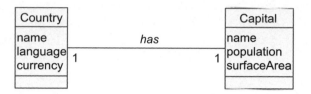

Figure 4.15 "Natural" solution

In order to continue with this simple solution, we can wonder – and rightly so – if the association is not an aggregation, indeed a composition? Yes, a country has a capital, and aggregation evokes capacity in the cartographical sense. Can we now go further and speak of composition?

Figure 4.16 Refined "natural" solution

A capital belongs to a country, and only one at that: this verifies the first criterion of the composition. But what happens if a country is destroyed? If the capital is also destroyed, then this is composition; but if not, it is only an aggregation. Here, we are dealing with a difficulty arising from the fact that the question does not make any reference to context, which would enable us to know how these concepts of country and capital are going to be used. Furthermore, "destroying" a country can just as easily mean its conquest during a war as its deletion from the database of our computer application... In the second case, composition is not disputable, whereas in the first, it is significantly less clear. Some thought is needed to understand that, here too, the capital disappears as an administrative concept, even if it is not physically destroyed. The diagram therefore takes account of this, as shown on Figure 4.16.

As a matter of fact, as we work through the sentences, we feel that we are missing a more general concept than capital: the notion of city. Let's assume that a country is annexed: its capital no longer exists as an administrative entity, but the city itself will not necessarily be destroyed! So, if we wish to define a more general model, it is interesting to model the fact that a capital is a city that plays a particular role within a country. An incomplete first solution is given below.

Figure 4.17   Insertion of the concept of city

It would be a pity not to take advantage of the insertion of the more general concept of city to express the fact that a country contains cities, of which only one plays the role of capital. We will therefore add a multiple aggregation between *Country* and *City*, and a constraint to demonstrate the fact that the capital of a country is inevitably one of its cities. The model now becomes markedly more sophisticated...

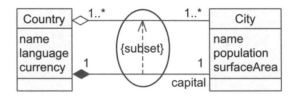

Figure 4.18   More complete solution with a constraint

Important: in our concern for generality, we have considered that a city can belong to several countries, and this also arms us against possible comments on the particular past or future status of towns, such as Berlin or Jerusalem... As a result, the relationship can only be one of aggregation.

Finally, if we want to make it clear that a capital is a city, but that it possesses specific properties, we must then make it a subclass and not a role, as shown on the diagram presented below. The <<refine>> dependency is there to indicate that the multiplicity of 1 to the side of *Country* on the composition with *Capital* replaces the less constraining multiplicity of "1..*" on the side of *Country* for cities. Note that UML 2.0 allows that generalisation may be applied to associations as well as to classes (even if most modelling tools do not...). So instead of the <<refine>> dependency, an alternate solution would have been to draw a generalisation from the composition "Country – Capital" to the aggregation "Country – City".

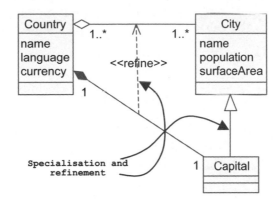

Figure 4.19 Solution with a concrete superclass

The *Capital* class can now receive additional attributes or associations, if the need arises.

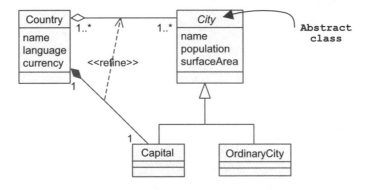

Figure 4.20 Solution with a concrete superclass

Compare the model we have just constructed with that of Figure 4.14. Both are correct, "legal" in UML and express the initial sentence in their own way. The first is very compact and simple to implement, but not very future-proof with regard to new demands of a user having to be met. The second is distinctly more complex to implement, but very flexible; it will last a long time in terms of having to develop to accommodate the needs of users. The choice between the two solutions must therefore be made on the basis of context: should we favour simplicity and deadlines for its construction, or, on the other hand, durability and possibilities for further development?

Finally, we should note that the superclass *City* in Figure 4.19 is not an abstract class. This is coherent as it only possesses one subclass. Indeed, the aim of an abstract class is to factorise properties that are shared by several subclasses, and not just by one! Nevertheless, a more complex solution would entail making *City* abstract, and introducing a second subclass called *OrdinaryCity* (as in Figure 4.20)...

****   4.4   Propose a sophisticated solution that enables the following file management system to be modelled:

1.   The files, shortcuts and directories are contained in directories and have a name;

2.   A shortcut can involve a file or a directory;

3.   Within a given directory, a name can only identify one element (file, sub-directory or shortcut).

Answer 4.4

Let's begin by modelling each of the three sentences in turn.

1.   The files, shortcuts and directories are contained in directories and have a name.

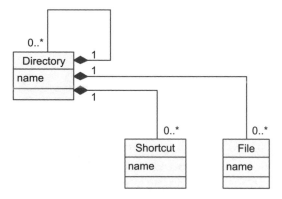

Figure 4.21   Modelling of sentence 1

Each of the three concepts must be represented by a class. The containment is modelled by a composition, as the multiplicity on the containing side is equal to 1, and the destruction of a directory brings about the destruction of everything that it contains.

Two associations in mutual exclusion convey the second sentence perfectly:

2.   A shortcut can involve a file or a directory.

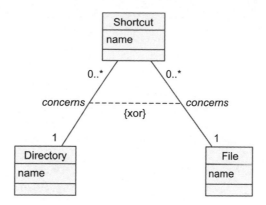

Figure 4.22 Modelling of sentence 2

Modelling becomes more complicated with the third sentence:

3. Within a given directory, a name can only identify one element (file, sub-directory or shortcut)..

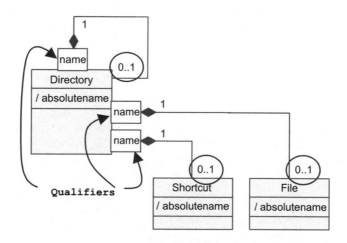

Figure 4.23 Modelling of sentence 3

The most obvious solution entails qualifying each of the three compositions with the name attribute. In fact, this qualifier represents the relative name of each element in its incorporated folder. We will note the reduction of the multiplicity on the other side of the qualifier. To model the absolute name, a derived attribute is entirely suitable, as it can be deduced from the succession of relative names.

What do you think of the following diagram, which brings together the models of the three sentences?

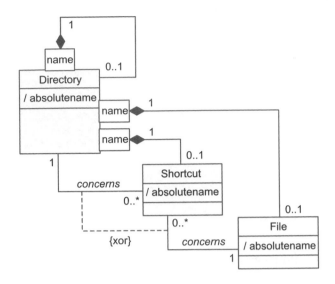

Figure 4.24 First version of the model

The model that we have obtained does seem to respond to the three sentences of the problem statement. However, it is not entirely correct! According to Figure 4.24, two files or two shortcuts cannot have the same name within an identical directory, but on the other hand, there is nothing stopping a file and a shortcut from having the same name...

This slight flaw actually brings a major problem to the fore: we need a single qualifier for every type of element contained within a directory and not a qualifier for each one. As it happens, we are taking three compositions into account: we therefore need to alter the model radically in order to have only one composition to qualify. How do we do this?

The solution is actually contained in the wording of the third sentence:

3. Within a given directory, a name can only identify one element (file, sub-directory or shortcut).

The word "element" must allow us to find the saving solution... What do directories contain? Files, shortcuts and other directories. Yes, but still, what do we call them all? Elements! If we add an abstract superclass, *Element*, which generalises the files, shortcuts and directories, the three compositions are reconciled into one with a single qualifier, and Bob's your uncle! Below is the resulting model:

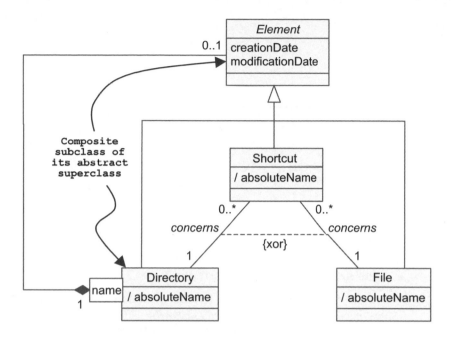

Figure 4.25 Final refined version

What is surprising about this solution, and what explains why it is not so easy to find, is the double asymmetrical relationship between the *Directory* and *Element* classes:

- *Directory* is a composite in relation to *Element*

- *Directory* is a subclass of *Element*.

The "composite" pattern

The solution demonstrated in the following figure has been described more generally in the reference work on *Design Patterns*,[37] under the name of "composite" pattern.

This pattern provides an elegant solution for the modelling of tree-like patterns that represent element/compound hierarchies. The client can thereby deal with individual objects (leaves) and their combinations (composites) in the same way.

37. *Design Patterns: Elements of Reusable Object-Oriented Software*, E. Gamma et al., Addison-Wesley, 1995.

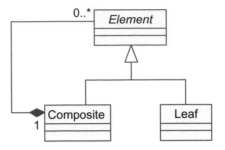

Generic model of "composite"

Case study 4 – Problem statement

We are going to resume the problem statement of the case study on training requests, which has already been dealt with from the functional view in Chapter 2. This time, we will reformulate it and simplify it slightly.

1. The training process is initialised when the training manager receives a training request on behalf of an employee.

2. This application is acknowledged by the person in charge who qualifies it and then forwards his or her agreement or disagreement to the person who is interested.

3. In the case of agreement, the person in charge looks in the catalogue of registered courses for a training course corresponding to the application.

4. He or she informs the employee of the course content and suggests a list of subsequent sessions to him or her.

5. When the employee sends back his or her choice, the training manager enrols the entrant in the session with the relevant training body.

6. The training manager subsequently checks the invoice that the training body has sent him or her before forwarding it to the bookkeeper of purchases.

We have already identified the business workers involved in the training process (Answer 2.6). We must now tackle the latter seen from the static view and try to discover the main business entities. For this, a lexical analysis of the text of the problem statement is highly recommended. In general, this technique is under used, as it can seem tedious. Nevertheless, it is very effective for discovering candidate objects in difficult cases, for example if the modeller knows very little about the business domain.

*   4.5   Model sentence 1 by using the stereotypes of the business modelling profile (as stated in Chapter 2).

Answer 4.5

We are going to carry out a detailed linguistic analysis of each sentence of the case study.

1.   The training process is initialised when the training manager receives a training request on behalf of an employee.

A simplistic analysis of nouns and noun phrases provides the following entities: training process, training manager, training request, employee. Let's consider each of the candidates in turn:

(a) *Training process* has already been identified in Chapter 2 as a business process: it will not appear on the class diagram.

(b) On the other hand, *training manager* and *employee* will feature on it, as they have been identified as business workers.

(c) Articles "a" or "the". The indefinite article ("a") is an indication that the name is being used generically, whereas the definite article ("the") is an indication that the name is unique in the context of the sentence. Be careful, though: the "a" article often means "a, in general" (as in: when the training manager receives *an* application for training), but sometimes also "one and only one" to indicate that the plural would not be possible (as in: on behalf of an employee). In this case, we obtain a multiplicity of 1 on an association.

We easily deduce the following class diagram from it.

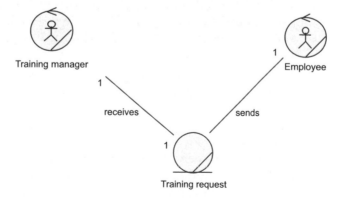

Figure 4.26 Static modelling of sentence 1

**   4.6   Model sentence 2.

Answer 4.6

Let's continue our linguistic analysis with the second sentence of the case study.

2.   This request is acknowledged by the person in charge, who qualifies it and then forwards his or her agreement or disagreement to the person who is interested.

By carrying out – as for the first sentence – a simplistic analysis of nouns and noun phrases, we obtain the following entities: request, person in charge, agreement, disagreement, person who is interested.

(d)   Indirect reference by "this", "these": a sentence using the word "this" almost always refers to the subject of the preceding sentence. The concepts of *application* and *training request* are therefore the same.

(e)   Be careful of synonyms! It is obvious that *person in charge* is not a new concept, but simply another form of *training manager*. It is not so obvious with the *person who is interested*, which refers to the employee who put forward the request.

(f)   Possessives: "his/her". We can convey possession in two ways: by an association or an attribute. We choose association if both the possessor and the possession are concepts. We choose attribute if the possession is a simple property of the possessor.

(g)   Coordinating conjunction, "or". An "or exclusive" must evoke a generalisation/specialisation relationship, but only if the specialised concepts have different attributes and behaviours. In the reverse case, it would be better to introduce a simple enumeration type. In our example, we can consider that agreement or disagreement are specialisations of a *response* entity relating to the request. Indeed, disagreement – unlike agreement – will probably have a *reason* attribute.

(h)   Verbs: the application is received by the person in charge, then acknowledged and finally qualified. There's no question of drawing three associations to model all the actions that the training manager can carry out with regard to the request. On the contrary, the class diagram must represent a static view, which is valid at any time. We will therefore rename the association between *Training manager* and *Training request* with a more neutral verb (*deals with*) and, consequently, modify the multiplicities.

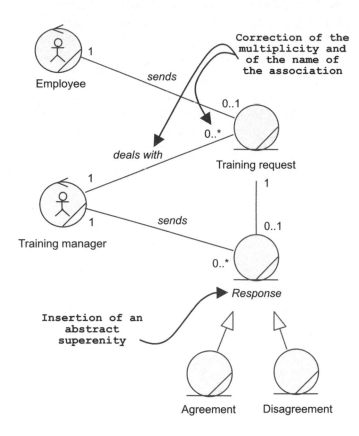

Figure 4.27   Static modelling of sentence 2

To complete the diagram, we have assumed that an employee cannot put forward more than one request at any one time. We will note the multiplicities between *Training request* and *Response*: a response is inevitabley linked to one and only one request; a request can exist without a response (as long as it is not acknowledged).

** 4.7   Model sentence 3.

Answer 4.7

3. In the case of agreement, the person in charge looks in the catalogue of registered courses for a training course corresponding to the application.

A new, quick analysis of nouns and noun phrases provides the following entities: agreement, person in charge, catalogue, training course, request.

(i) *Agreement, person in charge* and *request* were identified previously.

(j) Container and content: *catalogue* is a container formed from *training courses*; the two can give rise to entities if they bear attributes and behaviours. Such is the case in our example. We must therefore examine the possibility of an aggregation or a composition. Otherwise, the content may be a simple attribute of the container.

(k) Plural: the plural on a noun (catalogue *of* training course̲s) often gives rise to an entity in the singular, but with a multiplicity of "0..*" on an association.

(l) Verbs: be careful, as verbs often correspond to actions carried out on the entities (the person in charge *searches for...*). These actions are not generally conveyed in the analysis class diagram. However, they give information on the dynamics, and can give rise to sequence or collaboration diagram fragments.

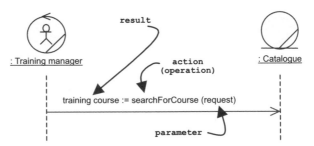

Figure 4.28   Dynamic model fragment of sentence 3

(m) Adjectives: these represent either attributes of an entity that has already been identified, or a possibility of a generalisation relationship. Watch out: they can also simply add "noise" to the text, as in our case where only *registered training courses* have a noteworthy existence in the training process.

(n) Present participles: these often indicate an association between two entities. For example, "a training course *corresponding to* the request" conveys the creation of an association between the *training course* and *request* entities.

(o) Watch out for synonyms! Synonyms are often used to avoid repetition, which makes the style heavy: *course* and *training course* are a good example of this. The modeller has to drive out these synonyms and "reduce" them by choosing a main entity name. We prefer the term *course* to *training course*.

All of these points result in the following class diagram.

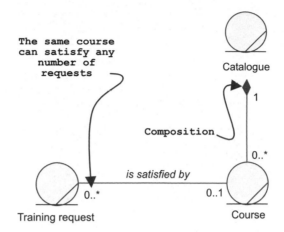

The same course can satisfy any number of requests

Catalogue

Composition

1

0..*

is satisfied by

0..*   0..1

Training request   Course

Figure 4.29   Static modelling of sentence 3

**   4.8   Model sentence 4.

Answer 4.8

4. He or she informs the employee of the course content and suggests a list of subsequent sessions to him or her.

A basic analysis of nouns and noun phrases enables the following entities to be noted down: employee, course, content, list, session.

(p) Indirect reference by a pronoun: "he/she", etc. Pronouns are references to another noun, which is often the subject of the preceding sentence. Here, "*he or she* informs ..." quite obviously concerns the person in charge.

(q) *Employee* and *course* were identified previously.

(r) Containment or possession: separate entity or attribute following the cases. If we consider that a course has a content whose structure is complex (prerequisites, objectives, detailed plan, etc.) and a behaviour, it is completely justified to make an entity of it. As we emphasised previously, we must examine the possibility of an aggregation or of a composition.

(s) Container: the word *list* simply indicates a multiplicity of "*" and often provides a notion of sequence (UML constraint of {ordered}). We should especially not identify a *list* entity at the time of the analysis stage: the choice of container types is really the responsibility of the detailed design, indeed that of the implementation.

(t) Watch out for false synonyms! This time, we must not think that *session* is a synonym of *course* or *training course*. The concept of *session* adds notions of date and location, which do not belong to the more generic concept of *course*. We can mention the merits of the "UML course in 4 days offered by Valtech", and enrol in the "session which takes places in Toulouse from 5 to 8 January 2004". Moreover, these entities have very distinct behaviours: we can defer or cancel a *session*, without modifying *course* in any way.

(u) Verbs: here again, the verbs represent exchanges of messages between instances, and definitely not associations.

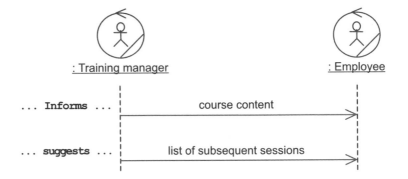

Figure 4.30 Dynamic model fragment of sentence 4

The result of these considerations is summarised in Figure 4.31.

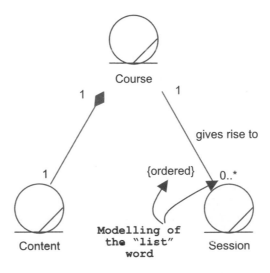

Figure 4.31 Dynamic model fragment of sentence 4

N.B. The relationship between *course* and *session* is a new illustration of the important "metaclass pattern", which was studied in Chapter 3, Answer 3.11.

*** 4.9 Model sentence 5.

Answer 4.9

5. When the employee sends back his or her choice, the training manager enrols the entrant in the session with the relevant training body.

Once again, the linguistic analysis provides us with the candidate entities: employee, choice, training manager, entrant, training body.

(v) *Employee*, *training manager* and *training body* were identified previously.

(w) Once again, we must see to it that we do not model a dynamic behaviour in the class diagram! Sentence 5 would be conveyed directly by the following sequence diagram fragment:

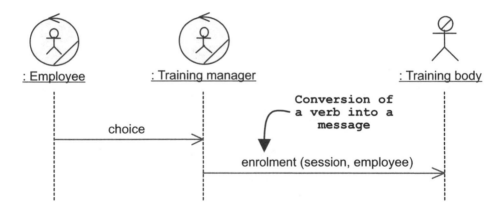

Figure 4.32 Dynamic modelling of sentence 5

(x) Verbs: the verb is often hiding a noun! In the previous example, where "the training manager *enrols* the entrant", the sequence diagram makes an *enrolment* message bearing parameters appear. In fact, we need an *enrolment* entity that represents a kind of contract between the training manager and the external body. This entity bears attributes (date, cost, etc.) and behaviours (deferral, cancellation, etc.). N.B. The entities of *contract* type are modelled very frequently as association classes.

(y) Vague terms: *choice* is a tricky word to model. This is an imprecise word, a vague term. We must therefore place it in the context to which it refers. According to sentence 4, the employee chooses one of the sessions offered by the training manager. In this context, the word *choice* is only used to identify a particular *session*, for which the training manager will make a request for enrolment with the training body. This is therefore not a new entity, but rather a role played by a session in connection with an enrolment.

(z) Roles: we must see to it that we do not create new entities systematically. Indeed, some nouns simply represent roles played by entities that have already been identified. Such is the case for *entrant*, which only describes a role played by an employee within the context of a session.

(aa) Actors. Should we link *training body* to *session*? This is what sentence 5 seems to indicate. However, we have seen with sentence 4 that sessions all refer to a course. It is therefore more sensible to link *training body* directly to *course*.

Static modelling of sentence 5 is illustrated on Figure 4.33.

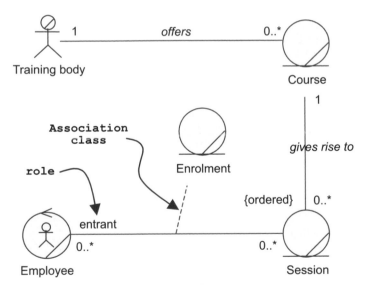

Figure 4.33 Static modelling of sentence 5

**   4.10 Model sentence 6.

Answer 4.10

6. The training manager subsequently checks the invoice that the training body has sent him or her before forwarding it to the bookkeeper of purchases.

For this last sentence, too, the linguistic analysis provides us with the candidate entities: training manager, subsequently, invoice, training body, bookkeeper of purchases.

(bb) *Training manager* and *training body* were identified previously. *Bookkeeper of purchases* is a business worker, as we stated in Chapter 2.

(cc) Temporal clauses: these are only used for dynamic modelling. In our case, "*subsequently* checks..." only marks the indication of a temporal succession of messages. It implicitly allows *invoice* to be linked to *enrolment* (cf. sentence 5).

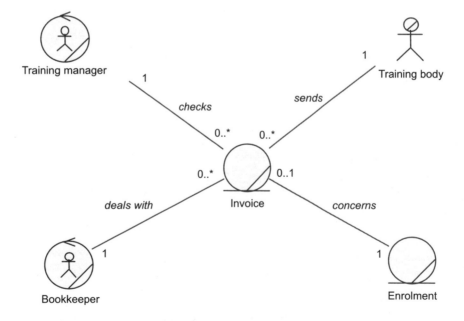

Figure 4.34 Static modelling of sentence 6

** 4.11 Unite all the preceding fragments in one class diagram.

Propose a division of the model into packages, which represent business organisation units.

Answer 4.11

The preliminary static model of our case study is the result of bringing together all the previous diagrams.

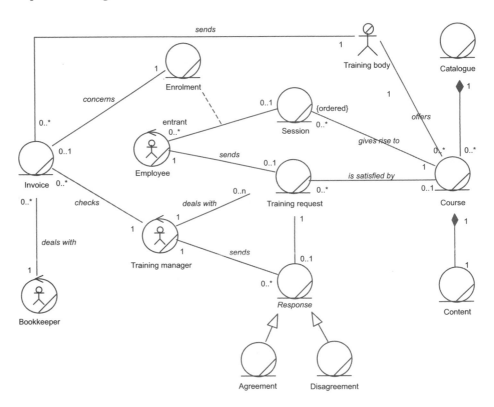

Figure 4.35 Preliminary static modelling of case study 4

How do we go about dividing this model into business organisation units?

- It is clear that the entire right section of the model (including the *session* entity) concerns the course catalogue and forms a coherent unit, which is relatively stable.

- The *invoice-bookkeeper* pair is also relatively independent from the others, and moreover, corresponds to a well-identified service of the company.

- The remaining parts of the model are the responsibility of the training manager and form a coherent set, which is focused on the training request.

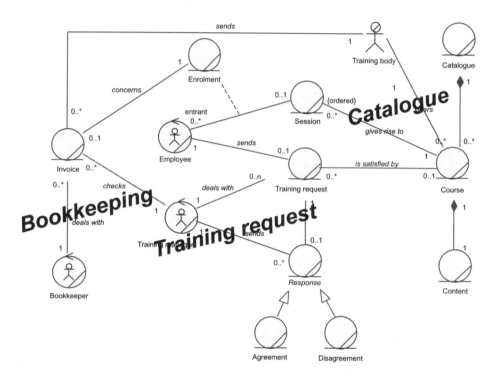

Figure 4.36 Division of the static model of case study 4

We can represent this structuring by dividing the preceding diagram, then displaying it as stereotyped packages, as shown in Chapter 2.

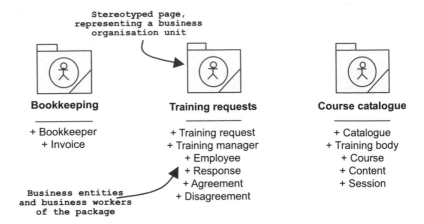

Figure 4.37 Stereotyped packages representing the division of the model

*** 4.12 Draw a class diagram for each organisation unit by attempting to minimise the dependencies between packages.

Add a few relevant business attributes to complete the static business model.

Answer 4.12

We will begin by studying the dependencies between the three packages that we identified in the previous exercise.

It is clear that the *Course catalogue* package can be autonomous, and that it can therefore form a reusable business element. It is also logical to make the invoice depend on the training request, rather than the other way round. The diagram of dependencies between business organisation units that we obtain is shown below; it respects the sacrosanct principles of dependencies between packages:

- No mutual dependencies

- No circular dependencies.

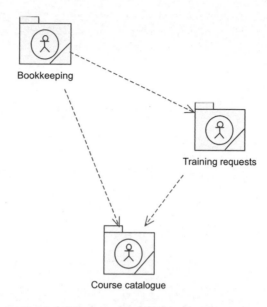

Figure 4.38 Desirable dependencies between business packages

This aim of dependencies between packages imposes a constraint on the navigability of the associations that traverse two organisation units, as indicated in the following way:

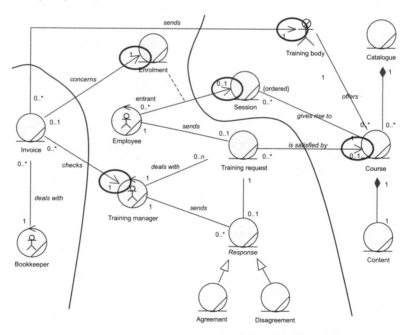

Figure 4.39 Addition of navigabilities on the associations that traverse two packages

By adding a few relevant business attributes, we can now draw a class diagram by package. Note that we represent also linked classes belonging to other packages (with the mention "from packageName"[38]).

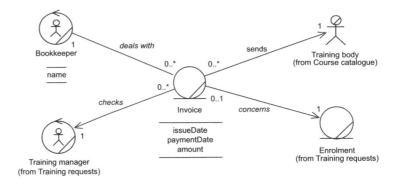

Figure 4.40 Class diagram of the Bookkeeping package

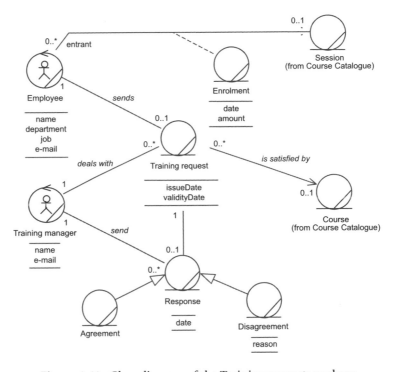

Figure 4.41 Class diagram of the Training requests package

---

38. This efficient graphical convention, though not a standard UML one, is implemented by Rational/Rose.

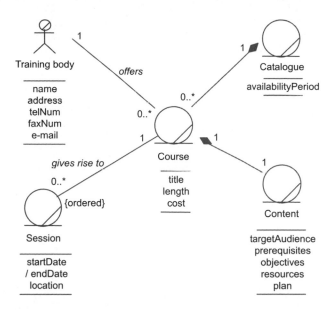

Figure 4.42 Class diagram of the Course catalogue package

Note the derived attribute, */endDate* of *Session*. The constraint could be written simply in OCL (the Object Constraint Language which is part of the UML specification[39]) as {self.endDate = self.startDate + course.length}.

---

39. For more information, refer to the OMG's Web site, where you can find the following recent document about UML 2.0 OCL: ad/2003-01-07.

Glossary & tips

This appendix comprises a thematic glossary of the static view (mainly inspired by the one found in the UML 2.0 Specifications from OMG), as well as a summary of tips, which have been taken from the two previous chapters.

Glossary

Abstract class	Class that cannot be directly instantiated and which is only used for specification.
Aggregation	Special form of association that specifies a whole-part relationship between the aggregate (whole) and a component part.
Association	Relationship between classifiers (classes, use cases, etc.), which describes a set of links.
Association class	Model element that has both association and class properties. An association class can be seen as an association that also has class properties, or as a class that also has association properties.
Attribute	A structural feature of a classifier that characterises instances of the classifier. An attribute relates an instance of a classifier to a value or values through a named relationship.
Business entity	Stereotyped class that represents a passive entity, which is used by a business worker (within the context of business modelling).
Business modelling	Modelling of the processes, resources and organisation of a company.
Business worker	Stereotyped class that represents a human acting within the organisation (within the context of business modelling).
Class	Classifier that describes a set of objects that share the same specifications of features, constraints and semantics.

Composition	Strong form of aggregation which requires that a part instance be included in at most one composite at a time, and that the composite object is responsible for the creation and destruction of the parts. Composition may be recursive.
Concrete class	In contrast with an abstract class, this is a class that can be instantiated in order to give objects.
Constraint	Semantic condition or restriction. It can be expressed in natural language text, mathematically formal notation, or a machine-readable language for the purpose of declaring some of the semantics of a model element.
Coupling	Dependency between model elements. "Coupling" represents a measure of the number of other classes, to which a given class is linked, which it knows about and on which it depends.
Dependency	Relationship between two modelling elements, in which a change to one modelling element (the independent element) will affect the other modelling element (the dependent element).
Derived attribute	An interesting attribute for the analyst, but redundant, as its value can be deduced from other information that is available in the model.
Generalisation	Relationship between classes where the children inherit the properties of their shared parent. However, each can incorporate additional specific properties, as well as modify the inherited operations.
Inheritance	Mechanism by which more specific elements incorporate structure and behaviour of more general elements.
Instance	An entity that has unique identity, a set of operations that can be applied to it, and state that stores the effects of the operations (an object is an instance of a class).
Interface	Named set of operations that characterise the behaviour of an element. Sometimes synonymous with specification or external view, or even public view.
Link	Semantic connection between objects by which an object can communicate with another object by means of sending messages.
Metaclass	A class whose instances are classes. Metaclasses are typically used to construct metamodels.

Metamodel	Model that defines the language for expressing a model.
Multiplicity	Specification of the range of allowable cardinalities that a set may assume. Multiplicity specifications may be given for association ends, parts within composites, repetitions and other purposes. Essentially a multiplicity is a (possible infinite) subset of the non-negative integers.
Navigability	Quality of an association that allows messages to flow from one class to another in a given direction.
Object	Entity with a well-defined boundary and identity that encapsulates state and behaviour; an object is an instance of a class.
Operation	Feature which declares a service that can be performed by instances of the classifier of which they are instances. Specification of a method.
Organisation unit	Stereotyped package that structures the business model (within the context of business modelling).
Package	General-purpose mechanism for grouping elements in UML, which can be used, for example, to organise classes and associations.
Pattern	Recurrent and well-researched modelling solution, which is applicable in a given context.
Private	Invisible from the exterior of a class (or of a package).
Public	Visible from the exterior of a class (or of a package).
Qualifier	An association attribute or tuple of attributes whose values partition the set of objects related to an object across an association.
Role	Synonym for association end often referring to a subset of classifier instances that are participating in the association.
Stereotype	A class that defines how an existing metaclass (or stereotype) may be extended, and enables the use of platform or domain-specific terminology or notation in addition to the ones used for the extended metaclass. Certain stereotypes are predefined in the UML, others may be user defined. Stereotypes are one of the extensibility mechanisms in UML.
Subclass	In a generalisation relationship, the specialisation of another class, the superclass.

Superclass	In a generalisation relationship, the generalisation of another class, the subclass.
Visibility	An enumeration whose value (public, protected or private) denotes how the model element to which it refers may be seen outside its enclosing namespace.

Tips

- The notion of state must not appear directly as an attribute on class diagrams: it will be modelled in the dynamic view by means of the state diagram. In the UML class diagram, the only available dynamic concepts are the operations.

- In object-oriented modelling, we consider that the object on which we will be able to realise a process has to have declared it as an operation. The other objects that will possess a reference on this object will then be able to send it a message invoking the operation.

- An object is a more "important" element than an attribute. A good criterion to apply can be set out as follows: if we can only ask an element for its value, then this is a straightforward attribute; if we can ask it several questions, though, it is an object that, in turn, possesses several attributes, as well as links with other objects.

- Do not hesitate to use the object diagram to give an example, or even a counterexample, that enables a tricky aspect of a class diagram to be refined.

- Only use the generalisation relationship when the subclass is 100% in accordance with the specifications of its superclass.

- UML naming convention:

  - Typically, you capitalise the first letter of every word in an attribute name except the first letter (unlike the names of classes, which systematically start with an upper case letter). The same conventions apply to the notation of association roles, as well as to operations.

- Use the concept of derived attribute to include attributes that can be computed from other elements, but that are shown for clarity even though they add no semantic information. Derived attributes allow the analyst not to make an overly premature decision with regard to design.

- It is recommended to use qualifiers without forgetting to modify the multiplicity on the other side of the association.

- Make sure that your classes do not have too many different responsibilities, for fear of violating a strong principle of object-oriented design known as *high cohesion*.

- If you identify an XX class that has too many responsibilities, and some of which are not specific to each instance, then consider the *metaclass pattern*. Add a *TypeXX* class, distribute the properties among the two classes and link these with a "* - 1" association. The *TypeXX* class is qualified as "metaclass", as it contains information that describes the *XX* class.

- For an aggregation to be a composition, we must confirm the following two criteria:

  - The multiplicity must not be greater than one on the side of the composite.

  - The lifetime of the parts must be dependent on that of the composite (particularly in the case of destruction).

- Make sure you know why a superclass is not always abstract (otherwise, we would not need visual help in the form of italics), and why the generalisation/specialisation relationship does not always lead to an inheritance "tree".

- Structuring a domain model is tricky to do. It has to rely on two basic principles: *coherence* and *independence*. The first principle consists in grouping classes that are related from a semantic point of view. In this respect, we must look for homogeneity at the level of the following criteria: objective, stability and lifetime. The second principle is to minimise dependencies between packages.

- The problem of associations that traverse two packages stems from the fact that just one of them is enough to lead to a mutual dependency if it is bidirectional. However, it is possible to limit this navigation to only one of the two directions in order to eliminate one of the two dependencies induced by the association. UML allows us to represent this navigability explicitly by adding an arrow on the association, which indicates the only direction possible.

- For a package to really be a reusable component, it must not depend on other packages.

- Respect the sacrosanct principles of dependencies between packages:

  - No mutual dependencies

  - No circular dependencies.

- An analysis package generally contains fewer than 10 classes.

- Be aware of the highly subjective character of modelling, and of the often difficult choice that you must make between simplicity and flexibility. A very compact model that is simple to implement will not be very future-proof when new demands are made by users. A model that is distinctly more complex to implement, but which is very flexible, will be better at developing in order to accommodate the needs of users. The choice between the two solutions must therefore be made on the basis of context: should we favour simplicity and deadlines for its construction, or, on the other hand, durability and possibilities for further development?

- Learn to identify appropriate times when it is advisable to use a modelling pattern. Make yourself study them intently so that you do not reinvent the pattern with each new model!

- Do not overlook the lexical analysis technique, even if it is generally under used as it can seem tedious. It is nevertheless very effective for discovering candidate objects in difficult cases; for example, if the modeller does not know much about the business domain in question.

- Some fundamental rules for lexical analysis:

  - Look for nouns and nominal groups to identify classes.

  - The indefinite article ("a") is an indication that the noun is used generically, whereas the definite article ("the") is an indication that the name is unique in the context of the sentence. In this case, we obtain a multiplicity of 1 on an association.

  - A sentence using the word "this" almost always refers to the subject of the preceding sentence.

  - Watch out for synonyms!

  - Possession can be conveyed in two ways: by an association or an attribute. Choose association if both the possessor and the possession are concepts. Choose attribute if the possession is a simple property of the possessor.

  - An "or exclusive" must evoke a generalisation/specialisation relationship, but only if the specialised concepts have different attributes and behaviours. In the reverse case, it is better to introduce a simple enumeration type.

  - The plural on a noun often gives rise to an entity in the singular, but with a multiplicity of "0..*" on an association.

- It is necessary to take into account that verbs often correspond to actions that are carried out on the entities. These actions are not generally conveyed in the analysis class diagram. However, they give information on the dynamics, and can give rise to sequence or collaboration diagram fragments.

- Make sure that you do not try to model dynamic behaviour in the class diagram!

- Adjectives: these represent either attributes of an entity that has already been identified, or a possibility of a generalisation relationship. Watch out: they can also simply add "noise" to the text.

- You must be careful not to create new entities systematically. Indeed, some nouns represent only roles played by entities that have already been identified.

- Present participles: these often indicate an association between two entities.

- Pronouns are references to another noun that is often the subject of the preceding sentence.

- The choice of container types is really the responsibility of the detailed design, indeed that of the implementation.

- You must always bear in mind that the class diagram has to represent a static view which is valid at any time. This particularly affects the multiplicities of associations.

Part 3

Dynamic view

Case study: coin-operated pay phone

Aims of the chapter

By working through a new case study, this chapter will allow us to illustrate, step by step, the main UML concepts and diagrams for the dynamic view.

Starting with actors and use cases, we will draw first a system sequence diagram. Then we will realise a specific kind of collaboration diagram, that we call dynamic context diagram, to list all the messages that the actors can send to the system and vice versa.

After this preliminary work, we will embark upon an in-depth description of the dynamics of the system. We will thus pay particular attention to the state diagram, which is, in our opinion, under used far too often, despite being an extremely useful diagram for describing complex behaviours accurately. We will explain in depth the following advanced concepts:

- Internal event "when"

- Superstate and substates

- Self-transition vs. internal transition

- Pseudostate "history"

- Send message

Elements involved

- Actor

- Use case, scenario

- System sequence diagram

- Dynamic context diagram

- Message

- State diagram

- State, transition, event

- Condition, action, activity.

Case study 5 – Problem statement

This case study involves a simplified system of a coin-operated pay phone.

1. The minimum cost of a call is 20 pence.

2. After inserting the coins, the user has 2 minutes to dial a number (this time limit is enforced by the switchboard[40]).

3. The line may be free or engaged.

4. The caller may hang up first.

5. The pay phone uses up money as soon as the callee picks up the receiver and with each unit of time (UT) generated by the switchboard.

6. The caller can add more coins at any time.

---

40. We use the word switchboard but it represents in fact the entire telephone network, also known as PSTN (Public Switched Telephone Network).

7. After hanging up, any unused change is returned.

From these seven sentences, we will progressively work through the following tasks:

- Identify the actors and use cases

- Construct a system sequence diagram

- Construct the dynamic context diagram

- Develop the state diagram of the pay phone.

5.1   Step 1 – Identifying the actors and use cases

First of all, we will identify the actors and use cases of the coin-operated pay phone.

** 5.1   Draw the use case diagram of the coin-operated pay phone.

Answer 5.1

What are the external entities that interact directly with the pay phone?

If we carry out a linguistic analysis (cf. Chapter 4) of the exposition, we will obtain the following five candidates: user, switchboard, caller, pay phone, callee.

Let's eliminate pay phone straight away as this concerns the system itself. On the other hand, the switchboard is actually an actor (non-human) that is connected directly to the system.

The only difficulty involves the human actors: user, caller and callee. As the first two terms appear to be synonyms, we can keep the word *callee* and, to make things symmetrical, rename user *caller.*

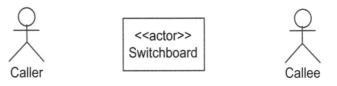

Figure 5.1   Preliminary list of the actors

How do the actors use the pay phone? The only usage that is really interesting in our context is that of the caller who telephones the callee. The switchboard acts as an intermediary between the two. If we refine our analysis even more, we quickly realise that the callee does not interact directly with the pay phone: he or she is completely concealed by the switchboard.

A graphical illustration of this problem of establishing boundaries is shown on the following static context diagram.

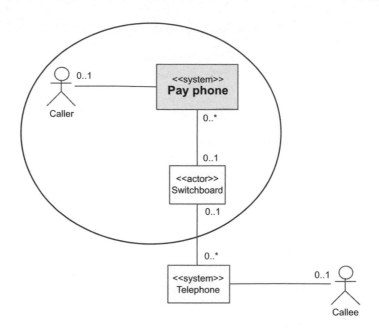

Figure 5.2 Extended static context diagram of the pay phone

It is plain to see on the preceding diagram that the caller communicates with the callee by means of three connected systems: the pay phone, the switchboard and the telephone of the callee. Note the symmetry of the diagram compared with the switchboard, which plays the role of actor with regard to the other two systems of the same kind.

The callee is therefore an indirect actor with regard to the pay phone. We will not keep it for our use case diagram that is ultimately very simple.

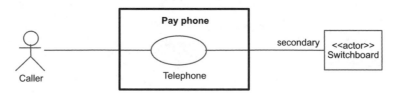

Figure 5.3 Use case diagram of the pay phone

5.2 Step 2 – Realising the system sequence diagram

Before immersing ourselves in the mysteries of the state diagram of the pay phone, we will prepare for it by creating a system sequence diagram first of all. In Chapters 1 and 2, we saw the relevance of this type of diagram and the different details that concern it.

** 5.2 Create a system sequence diagram that describes the main success scenario of the *Telephone* use case.

Answer 5.2

By using our knowledge of the field as our basis, we will describe an example of successful communication between a caller and a callee.

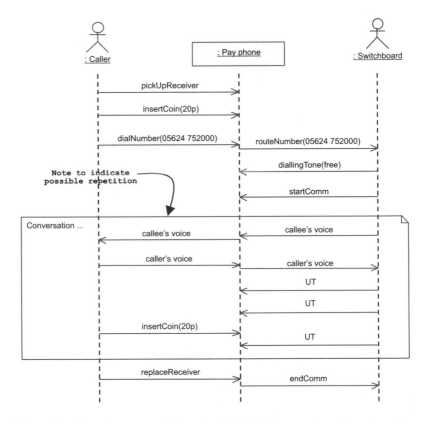

Figure 5.4 System sequence diagram of the *Telephone* main success scenario

As explained in Chapters 1 and 2, we use the following graphical conventions:

- The primary actor *Caller* to the left
- An object representing the *pay phone* in the middle
- The secondary actor *Switchboard* to the right.

We have not yet represented the replies from the pay phone to the caller (for example, in terms of dialling tone), as we do not want to make this first diagram cumbersome.

*** 5.3 Extend the preceding system sequence diagram with interesting internal activities and a few replies from the pay phone to the caller.

However, omit the conversation now so that you can concentrate on the "system operations".

Answer 5.3

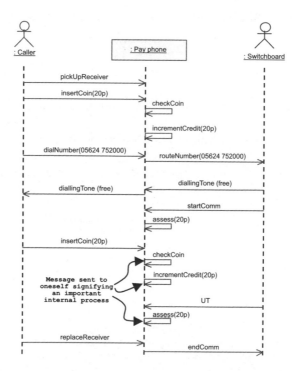

Figure 5.5 Completed system sequence diagram of the *Telephone* main success scenario

We have added important internal activities of the pay phone to the preceding diagram, such as checking the coins and managing the balance of the caller:

- Incrementation when inserting coins

- Decrementation when communication has begun and with each UT.

5.3   Step 3 – Representing the dynamic context

In order to round off the preparation for the state diagram, we will now list all the messages that are sent and especially those that are received by the pay phone. The messages received will become events that trigger transitions between states, and the messages sent will result in actions on the transitions.

The system sequence diagram created in step 2 lists quite a number of messages. We are now aiming for thoroughness and "genericness". For this objective, we advocate the graphical representation of the set of messages exchanged by the system with its actors by using a diagram that we call a *dynamic context diagram*.[41]

Graphical representation of the dynamic context

Use a *collaboration* diagram as follows:

- the system studied is represented by an object in the centre of the diagram;

- this central object is framed by an instance of each actor;

- a link connects the system to each of the actors;

- on each link, all input and output messages of the system are listed without numbering.

---

41.   As for the static context diagram, advocated in Chapter 1, this is not a conventional UML diagram, but it proved useful many times on real projects.

***   5.4   Create the dynamic context diagram of the pay phone by following the aforementioned steps.

Answer 5.4

On the basis of the two system sequence diagrams, we have listed the messages exchanged between the system and its actors. We then generalised them by adding parameters when required:

- InsertCoin (20p) becomes a parameterised message: "insertCoin(c)";

- dialNumber (05624 752000) becomes "dialNumber(num)";

- diallingTone (free) becomes "diallingTone(type)" to account for when the line is busy, etc.

This first task gives the following preliminary diagram:

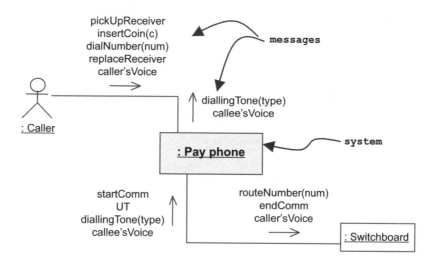

Figure 5.6   Preliminary version of the dynamic context diagram

Nevertheless, let's be careful not to forget that we started from the system sequence diagram that represents a main success scenario of the *Telephone* use case. Other messages can be considered between the pay phone and its actors:

- if there are coins that have not been used when the caller hangs up, the pay phone gives them back to him or her;

- after inserting the minimum amount of 20p, the pay phone sends a message to the switchboard for the deduction of the 2 minute time limit;

- if the number that has been dialled is not valid, the switchboard detects it;

- if the callee hangs up first, the end of communication is indicated by the switchboard;

- more generally, the switchboard sends the state of the line to the pay phone (free, engaged, out of order, etc.), and not just the type of dialling tone.

The dynamic context diagram is therefore completed, as shown on the following figure.

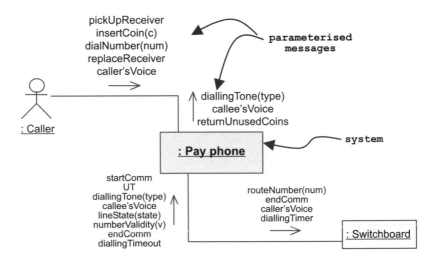

Figure 5.7   Full version of the dynamic context diagram

5.4   Step 4 – In-depth description using a state diagram

After all this preliminary work, we can now embark upon an in-depth description of the dynamics of the pay phone. To this end, UML has gone back to the well-known concept of *finite state machine*, that consists in taking an interest in the lifetime of a generic instance in the course of its interactions with the rest of the domain, in all possible cases. This local view of an object, which describes how it responds to events according to its current state and how it enters into a new state, is represented graphically in the form of a *state diagram*.

The behaviour of the pay phone is not commonplace, as is attested by the high number of messages identified on the dynamic context diagram, for example. In this case, we recommend an iterative and incremental approach.

Procedure for constructing state diagrams

- first of all, represent the sequence of states that describes the nominal behaviour of an instance, together with the transitions that are associated with it;

- progressively add the transitions that correspond to the "alternative" or error behaviours;

- complete the actions on the transitions and activities in the states;

- structure the diagram into substates and use advanced notation (`entry`, `exit`, etc.) if it becomes too complex.

This is the procedure that we will implement by means of the following questions.

**   5.5   Construct an initial state diagram that describes the main success behaviour of the coin-operated pay phone, adapted from the system sequence diagram.

Answer 5.5

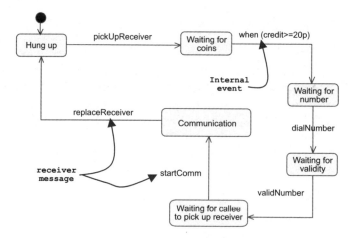

Figure 5.8   First version of the state diagram

For the *Telephone* use case, the nominal initial state of the pay phone is at "hung up". When the caller picks up the receiver, he or she must then insert a minimum of 20p to be able to dial his or her number. Once a valid number is dialled, the pay phone waits for the reply from the switchboard, then the callee picks up the receiver. The conversation is then continued until one of the two hangs up. The pay phone then returns to its initial state.

Let's convey this text as an initial state diagram skeleton (see Figure 5.8).

Internal event: « when »

We will notice that the majority of events that trigger transitions between states correspond to the receipt of a message sent by an actor. Moreover, we have used the same names for the events as for the corresponding messages (except for *validNumber* which is simpler to read than the strict *numberValidity(true)*).

Only the change of the "Waiting for coins" state into the "Waiting for number" state is produced by an internal event in the pay phone: the detection of when the amount of 20p is satisfied. UML offers a keyword to distinguish these changes in internal states: «when», followed by a Boolean expression, whose change from false to true triggers the transition.

***   5.6   How do we represent the fact that the caller can hang up at any time, and not only in the communication state?

Answer 5.6

As is often the case, there are two ways to go about this: the basic and the sophisticated! The basic solution involves adding transitions triggered by the *replaceReceiver* event and exiting all the states in order to arrive at the "Hung up" state. But the diagram suddenly appears rather "busy" then...

The sophisticated solution involves inserting a composite state, "Picked up receiver", which enables factorisation of the output transition towards the "Hung up" state.

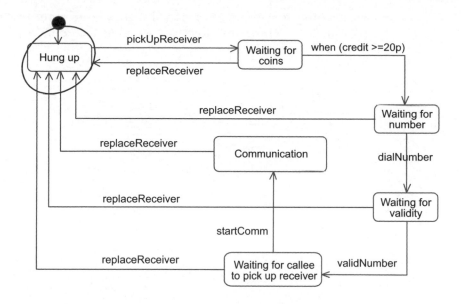

Figure 5.9 Basic solution

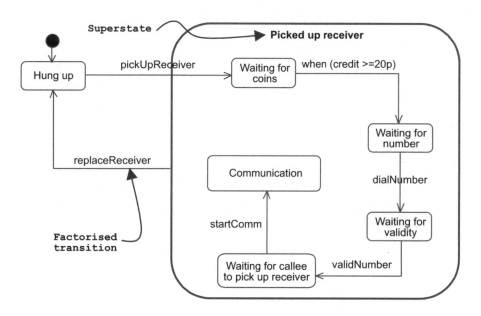

Figure 5.10 Sophisticated solution

We will also note that we could have used slightly more sophisticated notation for the transition of "Hung up" towards "Waiting for coins", as shown on the following diagram.

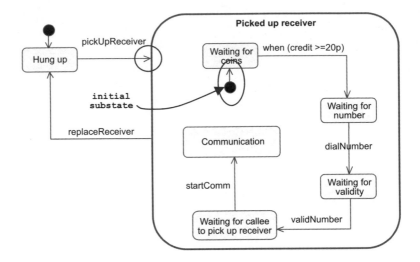

Figure 5.11 Sophisticated solution with initial substate

Instead of having a transition directly between "Hung up" and "Waiting for coins", we obtain a first transition between "Hung up" and "Picked up receiver", then the graphical symbol of the initial state within "Picked up receiver" in order to give an explicit indication of the initial substate. This method of proceeding enables the division of the state diagram into two levels:

- a first level, which only makes the "Hung up" and "Picked up receiver" states appear;

- a second level, which corresponds to the breakdown of "Picked up receiver".

In order to retain a level of simplicity, we will keep the direct transition in the follow-up of the case study.

**** 5.7   How can the credit of the caller reach 20p?

Consider several solutions.

Answer 5.7

For the time being, the credit of the caller only occurs in the Boolean expression associated with the internal event of « when ». However, for the credit to reach 20p, the caller must insert one or more coins.

We can therefore place a self-transition (which returns towards the source state) on the "Waiting for coins" state. As soon as the credit exceeds 20p, the pay phone has to enter the "Waiting for number" state.

If we only want to use events caused by the receipt of messages, we will probably insert conditions on the transitions, as illustrated on the following diagram.

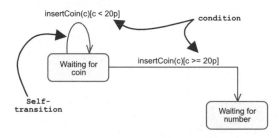

Figure 5.12   First incorrect solution

This solution, which seems obvious, is nevertheless incorrect as it does not allow the user to dial a number after having inserted two 10p coins... The pay phone must therefore store a *credit* attribute that is incremented each time a coin is inserted.

It is tempting to alter our diagram by adding an action and by modifying the conditions:

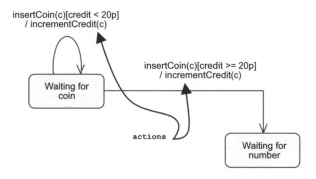

Figure 5.13   Second incorrect solution

Alas, this solution is also incorrect, but in a more subtle way! The semantics of a transition in UML is as follows: when the trigger event is produced, the condition is tested; if the condition is valued at true, the transition is fired and the associated action is then realised.

Let's see how this actually happens by applying it to our example, starting from "Waiting for coins" with an initial credit of 0p:

- The caller inserts a 10p coin. The credit is less than 20p (it is still worth 0p): the self-transition is triggered and the credit is now worth 10p.

- The caller inserts a 10p coin. The credit is less than 20p (it is worth 10p): the self-transition is triggered and the credit is now worth 20p.

The result is surprising: the caller has paid 20p and is still unable to dial his or her number... The moral of this statement is as follows: do not attempt to test an item of information in a condition before having modified it by an action. Such is the case when you want to communicate everything in a single transition.

We easily deduce the correct solution from this:

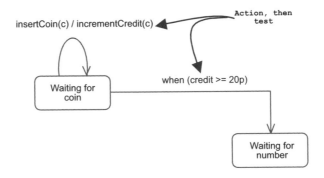

Figure 5.14   Correct solution

You should make a note of this method of modelling, as it can be reused in many contexts.

****   5.8   Complete the credit management of the caller.

Do not miss out the last sentence: the caller can add more coins at any time ...

Answer 5.8

Let's take things from the beginning again. Let's acknowledge that picking up the receiver might make coins fall that would have been inserted previously. The credit must therefore be initialised to "0" on this transition.

Next, the caller needs to insert one or more coins for the credit to reach 20p. We have therefore placed a self- transition on the "Waiting for coins" state. As soon as the credit exceeds 20p, the change transition « when » leads the pay phone to the "Waiting for number" state.

The credit amount does not change until the callee picks up the receiver, which is conveyed by the *startComm* message sent by the switchboard. From this moment on, the credit is decremented regularly, as is indicated by sentence 5 ("The pay phone uses up money as soon as the callee picks up the receiver and with each unit of time (TU) generated by the switchboard"). The *assess* action represents the fall of a coin each time one is inserted.

Finally, it must not forget to return unused coins when the caller hangs up.

If we account for all of these points, we obtain the following diagram.

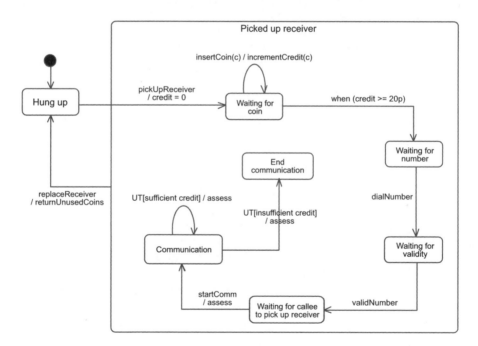

Figure 5.15 Accounting for credit management

We will take note of the new state, "End communication", which has been inserted to deal with the situation where communication is broken off by the pay phone due to lack of credit.

We still need to model the last sentence: the caller can add more coins at any time. Here again, several solutions are possible but only one will turn out to be both correct and sophisticated.

The first idea consists in inserting a self-transition – identical to that of "Waiting for coin" – on each substate of "Picked up receiver". This way of proceeding is correct, but its implementation is very cumbersome, and we would rather try to factorise by means of the composite state. Is it not possible to transfer the self-transition to the actual level of "Picked up receiver", as illustrated on the diagram below?

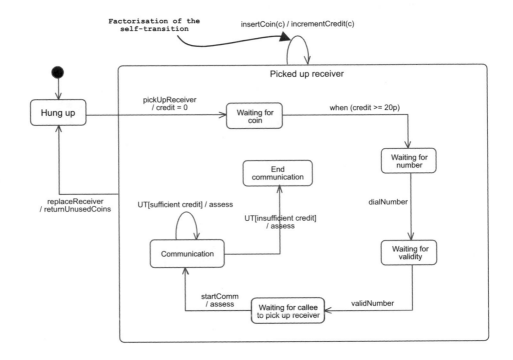

Figure 5.16   Incorrect solution

Alas, this solution is not satisfactory, as we will now discover.

Self-transition or internal transition?

In the case of a *self-transition*, the object leaves its source state in order to encounter it again. This can have not inconsiderable secondary effects, such as the interruption then re-starting of an activity, the realisation of entry actions (« entry ») or exit actions (« exit ») of the state, etc. Moreover, when a composite state is broken down into substates, a self-transition inevitably returns the object to the initial substate. Here, each insertion of a coin would return the pay phone to the "Waiting for coin" state, which is implicitly the initial substate of "Picked up receiver"!

To solve this present problem, the notion of *internal transition* exists in UML; it represents a pair (event/action) that has no influence on the present state. The internal transition is thus acknowledged within the symbol of the state.

This is the approach that we will use for our case study.

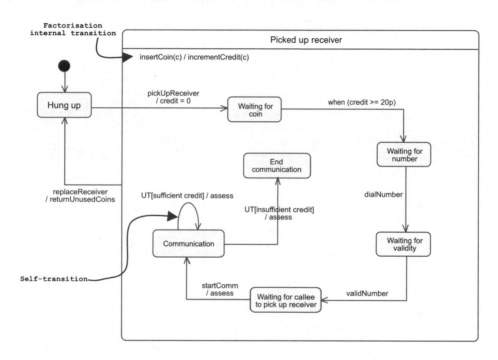

Figure 5.17 Correct solution with factorised internal transition

We would also like to note that, strictly speaking, the self-transition on the "Communication" state should also be an internal transition. In fact, when there is no secondary effect, we prefer to use the self-transition, which is more visual. However, we must be careful if we have to break down "Communication" into substates one day...

A second correct solution, but which is more complex, involves using the « history » pseudostate.

Pseudostate « history »

The activation of the pseudostate « history » allows a composite state to remember the last sequential substate that was active before an exiting transition. A transition towards the « history » state makes the last active substate active again, instead of returning to the initial substate.

Figure 5.16 can therefore be corrected as follows.

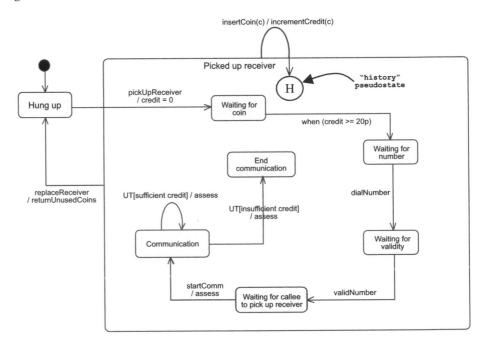

Figure 5.18 Correct solution with «history» pseudostate

***   5.9   Complete the state diagram to account for the whole problem statement.

Propose complements if you consider them to be necessary.

Answer 5.9

Let's go over the sentences of the problem statement again, one by one. We have dealt with sentences 1, 5 and 6 in detail. On the other hand, we have only partly accounted for sentences 2, 3 and 4.

Let's first take a look at sentence 2:

2. After inserting the coins, the user has 2 minutes to dial a number (this time limit is enforced by the switchboard).

As the time limit is enforced by the switchboard, we have inserted two messages in the context diagram (cf. Figure 5.7):

- *diallingTimer* sent by the pay phone to the switchboard;

- *diallingTimeout* sent by the switchboard to the pay phone.

Send message: « send »

UML introduced a keyword, `send`, to represent the important action that entails sending a message to another object when a transition is fired.

The syntax of this particular action is as follows: "/ `send` target.message". Be careful, as in earlier versions of UML the notation was more obscure: "^target.message".

In the state diagram of the pay phone, we will therefore have a transition that will be fired when the *diallingTimeout* message is received, and when the *diallingTimer* message is sent on entering the "Waiting for number" state, as shown on the following diagram.

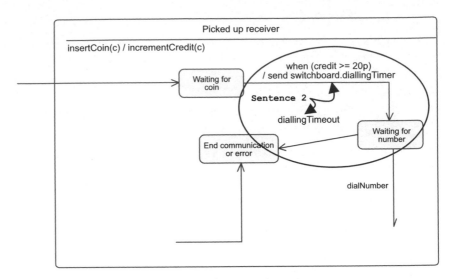

Figure 5.19   Modelling of sentence 2

It is important to note that we have renamed the "End communication" state, as this "sink state" (that is to say, not having any exit transition) will also be useful for all cases of error.

Let's now have a look at sentence 3:

3.   The line can be free or engaged.

Up to now, we have assumed that the line was free and that the callee picked up the receiver. We are going to introduce in the model not only the possibility that the switchboard sends back a line state (engaged), but also that the callee does not pick up the receiver (which was not anticipated explicitly in the exposition). For this last case, we assume that the switchboard sends a *callTimeout* message that leads the pay phone to the error state.

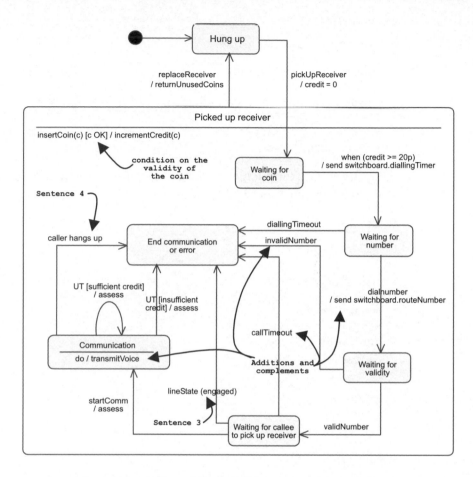

Figure 5.20 Full modelling of all sentences of the exposition

Sentence 4 simply adds a transition between the "Communication" and "End communication" states:

4. The caller can hang up first.

The completed state diagram is represented on Figure 5.20.

*** 5.10 By making use of this entire dynamic study, propose an extended version of the static context diagram that will display the attributes and operations of the pay phone class.

Answer 5.10

We will apply a few simple rules:

- Public operations correspond to the names of messages sent by the actors.

- Private operations correspond to the names of messages sent to oneself.

- Attributes correspond to the names of persistent data, manipulated in the actions or conditions.

Firstly, let's take a look at the public operations. According to the dynamic context diagram (cf. Figure 5.7), we can identify:

- pickUpReceiver

- insertCoin(c)

- dialNumber(num)

- replaceReceiver

- startComm

- UT

- lineState(state)

- numberValidity(v)

- endComm

- diallingTimeout

The state diagram (cf. Figure 5.20) leads us to add the following operation:

- callTimeout

Let's now go through the private operations. The completed system sequence diagram (cf. Figure 5.5) showed the following messages:

- checkCoin

- incrementCredit

- assess

On the state diagram, we inserted the "do / transmitVoice" activity, which can be added to the list of private operations (as it is triggered indirectly by arrival in the

"Communication" state). We will note that the *checkCoin* operation is conveyed by a "[c OK]" condition on the factorised internal transition.

Finally, what are the interesting attributes? It is clear that an important item of information is that which is managed continuously by the pay phone: *credit* of the caller. As a result, we can eliminate the implicit operations of reading/writing this attribute (*incrementCredit, assess*).

We now know enough to draw the extended static context diagram.

Extended static context diagram

An "extended static context diagram" is what we call a static context diagram in which we add attributes and operations of system level to the class that represents the system (conceived as a black box), as well as to non-human actors.

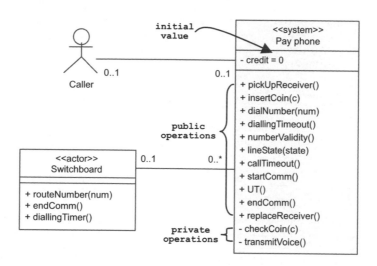

Figure 5.21 Extended context diagram

We will note that we have made the public operations appear on the non-human actor, *Switchboard,* but not on the *Caller* actor. The concept of operation does not make sense on a human actor: we do not generally try to model him or her in a deterministic way. On a non-human actor, though, the list of operations represents its interface (in the sense of an API, for example) as it is used by the system in question. This is particularly useful to check the interoperability of the two systems, and to make sure that these operations are already available, or planned in the specifications.

As regards UML notation, let's remember that:

- "-" means private

- "+" means public

- "=" allows the initial value of an attribute to be specified.

Bibliography

[Booch 99]	*The Unified Modeling Language User Guide*, G. Booch, J. Rumbaugh, I. Jacobson, Addison-Wesley, 1999.
[Douglass 00]	*Real-Time UML: Developing Efficient Objects for Embedded Systems* (2nd Edition), B. P. Douglass, Addison-Wesley, 2000.
[Freeman 01]	*Designing Concurrent Distributed and Real-Time Applications with UML*, P. Freeman, B. Selic, Addison-Wesley, 2001.
[Mellor 91]	*Object Lifecycles: Modeling the World in States*, S. Mellor, S. Shlaer, Prentice Hall, 1991.
[Mellor 02]	*Executable UML: A Foundation For Model-Driven Architecture*, S. Mellor, M. Balcer, Addison-Wesley, 2002.
[Roques 99]	Hierarchical Context Diagrams with UML: An Experience Report on Satellite Ground System Analysis, P. Roques, E. Bourdeau, P. Lugagne, in *<<UML>>'98: Beyond the Notation*, J. Bezivin & P. A. Muller (Eds), Springer Verlag LNCS 1618, 1999.
[Rumbaugh 91]	*Object-Oriented Modeling and Design*, J. Rumbaugh et al., Prentice Hall, 1991.
[Rumbaugh 99]	*The Unified Modeling Language Reference Manual*, J. Rumbaugh, I. Jacobson, G. Booch, Addison-Wesley, 1999.

Complementary exercises

Aims of the chapter

By working through several short exercises, this chapter will allow us to complete the overview of the main difficulties which are involved in constructing UML state diagrams, namely:

- Continuous or finite activity – completion transition

- Pseudo-event "after"

- Concurrent regions

- Entry/exit actions

- Inheritance of transitions from the superstate

- ...

We have already dealt with sequence diagrams in Chapters 1 and 2, and we will go over collaboration diagrams in the section dedicated to design.

Alarm clock

Let's consider a simplified alarm clock:

1. We can set the alarm to "on" or "off";

2. When the current time becomes that which is set on the alarm, the alarm clock rings continuously;

3. We can make the ringing stop.

** 6.1 Draw the corresponding state diagram.

Answer 6.1

Firstly, let's take a look at the first sentence:

1. We can set the alarm to "on" or "off".

The alarm clock clearly has two distinct states: *Unprepared* (alarm "off") or *Prepared* (alarm "on"). One action from the user enables it to change state. We assume that the alarm clock is unprepared at the start. Note the *alarmTime* parameter of the *prepare* event.

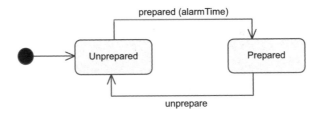

Figure 6.1 State diagram of sentence 1

Let's now look at the other two sentences:

2. When the current time becomes that which is set on the alarm, the alarm clock rings continuously;

3. We can make the ringing stop.

The occurrence of ringing forms a new state for the alarm clock. It involves a period of time, during which the alarm clock carries out a certain activity (ringing) that lasts until an event comes to stop it.

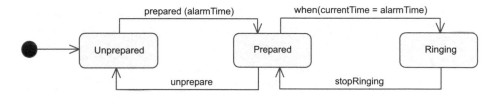

Figure 6.2 Preliminary state diagram of the alarm clock

The shift from the *Prepared* state to the *Ringing* state is triggered by a transition due to an internal change, represented by means of the « when » keyword. According to the problem statement, however, the return of the *Ringing* state to the *Prepared* state is only carried out on a user event.

***   6.2   Complete the preceding state diagram to account for the fact that the alarm clock stops ringing by itself after a certain amount of time.

Answer 6.2

There is therefore a second possibility of exiting the *Ringing* state: when the alarm clock stops ringing of its own accord after a certain amount of time.

Continuous or finite activity – completion transition

An activity within a state can be either:

- "continuous": it only stops when an event takes place that makes the object exit from the state;

- "finite": it can also be stopped by an event, but in any case, it stops by itself after a certain amount of time, or when a certain condition is met.

The completion transition of a finite activity, also known as *completion transition*, is represented in UML without an event name or a keyword (as in activity diagrams).

In our example, all we therefore need to do is add a *ring* activity to the *Ringing* state and a completion transition exiting this state. The completed state diagram is represented on the following figure.

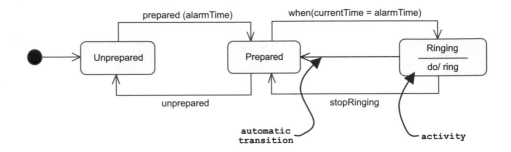

Figure 6.3   Completed state diagram of the alarm clock

It is a good idea to wonder if the user has the right to 'unprepare' the alarm clock whilst it is ringing. In this case, we would have to add a transition triggered by *unprepare* and going directly from *Ringing* to *Unprepared*.

** 6.3   Deduce from the aforementioned points the extended static context diagram of the alarm clock (cf. 5.10).

Answer 6.3

If we apply the rules again, which were stated in Answer 5.10, we easily obtain the diagram below.

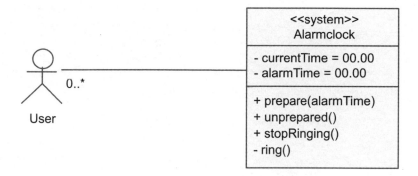

Figure 6.4 Extended static context diagram

Digital watch

Let's consider a simplified digital watch:

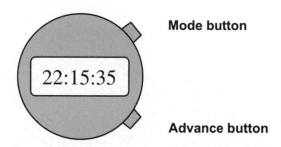

Figure 6.5 Simplified digital watch

1. The current mode is the "Display" mode;

2. When you press once on the mode button, the watch changes to "change hour". Every time you press the advance button, the hour is incremented by a unit;

3. When you press the mode button again, the watch changes to "change minute". Every time you press on the advance button, the minutes are incremented by a unit.

4. When you press the mode button a third time, the watch goes back to "Display" mode.

*   6.4   Draw the corresponding state diagram.

Answer 6.4

We easily obtain this typical state diagram, which is set out on the following figure.

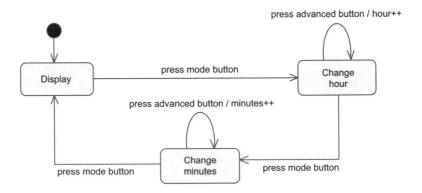

Figure 6.6 Preliminary state diagram of the digital watch

We can observe the notation in C++ or Java style that is used for the actions (to indicate that it is incremented by one): "hour++" and "minutes++". UML does not yet offer an action language; we can therefore express the detail of the actions as we wish: free text, pseudocode, etc.

We obtain self-transitions on the states for changes and not on the state for display. Does this mean that the "press advance button" event is impossible in the "Display" state? Of course not. Rather, this means that, as this event does not have any effect in this state, it does not trigger any transition. The event is purely and simply wasted.

* * * * 6.5 Add the following behaviour: when you press the advance button for longer than two seconds, the hours (or the minutes) are incremented quickly until the button is released.

Envisage several possible solutions.

Answer 6.5

In the preceding example, the events of pressing the buttons actually corresponded to the indivisible pair of "press" and "release". We had considered that the length of time spent pressing each button was trivial with regard to lengths of the states or, in any case, insignificant. With the new exposition, this is no longer the case, as the length of time spent pressing the advance button has an influence on the behaviour of the watch. The correct approach entails inserting a new event: "release advance button", in order to be able to manage the time spent pressing the button.

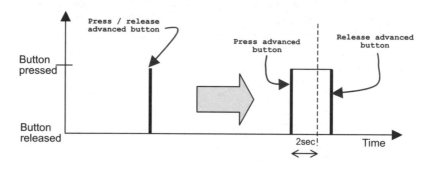

Figure 6.7 Conversion of an event into two

An initial and tempting solution consists in inserting a condition on the length of time spent pressing the button, as well as a new state called "Fast incrementation", as illustrated on Figure 6.8.

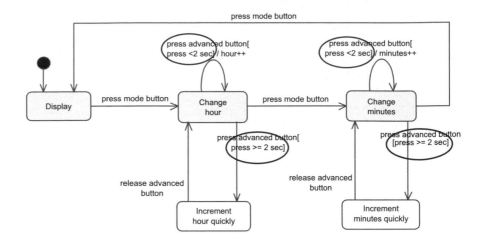

Figure 6.8 Incorrect modification of the state diagram of the digital watch

Yet, this seemingly obvious solution is not acceptable in UML.

Indeed, an event (such as a transition and an action) is instantaneous by convention, or in any case, indivisible (atomic). It is therefore completely inappropriate to test its length! The only dynamic concepts in UML, for which the notion of length is significant, are state and activity. We must therefore use these to solve this exercise. There are two possible solutions: both require the addition of an intermediary state so that we can test the length of time spent pressing the advance button, but they differ in the way that they carry out this test:

- The first approach involves inserting a finite activity, "wait 2 sec", in the intermediary state and a completion transition that represents the fact that the button is being pressed for longer than two seconds.

- The second approach consists in using another UML keyword: the pseudo-event, « after », followed by an amount of time in parentheses representing the term of a time expression.

In order to illustrate the two solutions, we have represented them together on the following diagram, but in reality, we would naturally have to choose just one of them and apply it to the two states of modification. As far as we are concerned, we recommend the second solution as it seems simpler and easier to read.

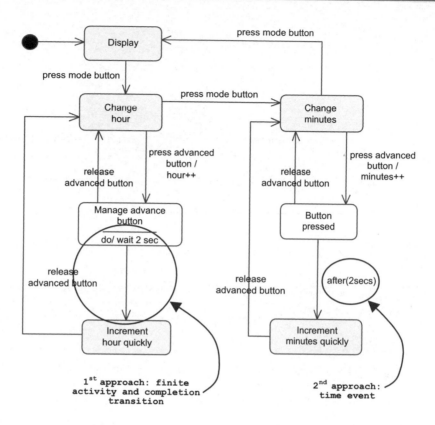

Figure 6.9 The two possibilities for implementing a correct modification of the state diagram of the digital watch

We will make a note of the fact that the initial behaviour is retained: if the advance button is released in less than two seconds, the hours (or minutes) are incremented by one unit. In fact, the self-transition that existed on each state for change was able to be divided into two following the separation of the two events, "press" and "release", and the addition of the intermediary state.

Let's go back to our digital watch example as it was set out at the beginning of the exercise, and now add a further two buttons to it:

- A light button; by pressing it, the watch face is lit until the button is released;

- An alarm button, which adds a standard feature to the digital watch, as described in the first exercise of this chapter (alarm clock).

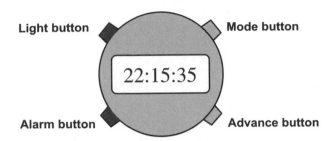

Figure 6.10 Completed digital watch

* * * *   6.6   Draw the full state diagram, including all behaviours of the watch.

Answer 6.6

It is plain to see that we have three concurrent behaviours:

- management of the display,

- management of the alarm,

- management of the light.

Let's start with the simplest one, which concerns managing the light. This can be modelled very simply by an automatic mechanism with two states, as is shown on the following diagram.

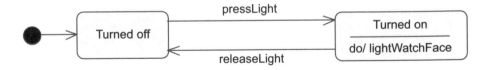

Figure 6.11 State diagram for managing the light

If management of the light can be modelled completely separately, then this does not work for the display and the alarm. We must now also be able to modify the hour and minute of the alarm, which adds two new states to the diagram in Figure 6.6, as shown below.

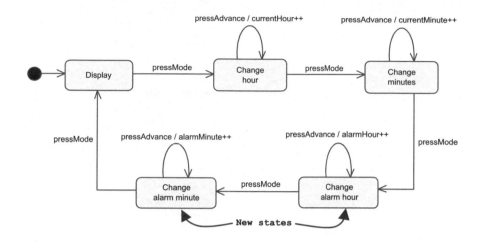

Figure 6.12 State diagram for managing the display

All we need to do now is model managing the alarm. We can look at the state diagram of the alarm clock (cf. Figure 6.3) to help us obtain the following diagram. Note the dependency with management of the display *via* the test carried out by management of the alarm on the attributes (« when »...).

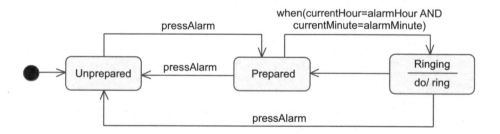

Figure 6.13 State diagram for managing the alarm

We have therefore obtained three state diagrams. How do we arrange things so that these three separate diagrams describe the behaviour of the digital watch?

Here again, two solutions are possible:

- Consider that every instance of Watch in fact contains three instances and that each one manages one of the three behaviours described previously. In this way, every watch delegates a part of its dynamics to a display, light or alarm instance, according to the case. We can represent this by means of a composition relationship in a class diagram.

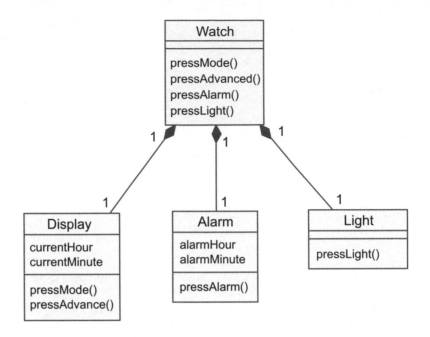

Figure 6.14   Class diagram that shows the composition relationship

- Describe "concurrent regions" within the state diagram of the Watch class. This solution is not used as often as the previous one (mainly because certain UML tools do not offer it), but it is just as feasible. The present state of the watch then becomes a three-lined vector: state of the display, state of the alarm, state of the lighting. A watch can simultaneously have its display in minute modification, be in the middle of ringing and have its face lit.

The state diagram of the watch would then look as follows in Figure 6.15.

We will note that each "region" has to be initialised as, if the states are exclusive within a concurrent region, they exist simultaneously in the three regions.

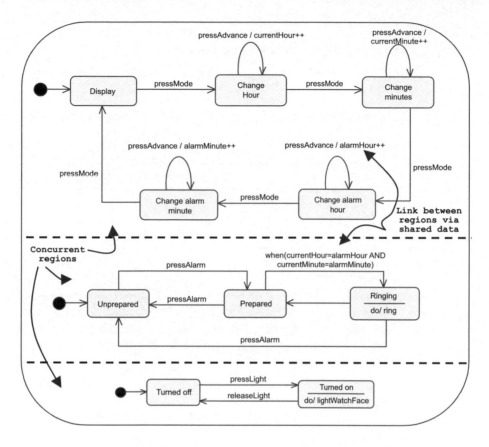

Figure 6.15 State diagram of the watch with concurrent regions

Complex hierarchical state diagram

Let's study the following state diagram fragment, which contains a number of actions.

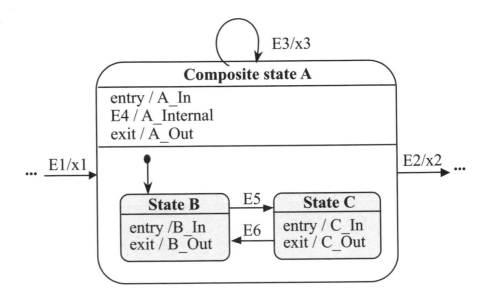

Figure 6.16 An example of a complex state diagram

Entry (or exit) action

An entry action (introduced by the `entry` keyword within the symbol of a state) represents an action that is executed each time this state is entered.

This enables us to share an identical action that will be triggered by all transitions that enter the same state.

The exit action (introduced by the `exit` keyword) is the corresponding action exiting the state.

The diagram of the problem statement therefore comprises:

- a self-transition on the composite state (E3/x3),
- an internal transition in the composite state (E4/A_Internal),
- entry and exit transitions in the composite state and each of the substates.

We are going to study the temporal order of execution of actions by completing the following table. We will start with the state on the left of the diagram symbolised by "...", and for each line of the table, we will consider the target state of the preceding line as the source state.

Source state	Event	Actions	Target state
...	E1	?	?
?	E5	?	?
?	E4	?	?
?	E6	?	?
?	E3	?	?
?	E5	?	?
?	E3	?	?
?	E2	?	?

***   6.7   Fill in the preceding table.

Answer 6.7

In the source state, symbolised by "..." on the left of the diagram, the E1 event triggers the x1 action, then leads to the A composite state. This entry in the A composite state triggers the entry action, A_In, then entry in the B substate (because of the symbol of the initial substate), and therefore the entry action, B_In.

Source state	Event	Actions	Target state
...	E1	x1, A_In, B_In	B (in A)

In the B state, the E5 event causes the object to exit the state and therefore triggers the B_Out action, then leads to the C state and, consequently, triggers the C_In action.

Source state	Event	Actions	Target state
B	E5	B_Out, C_In	C (in A)

Is the E4 event possible in the C state? Yes, as the internal transitions are inherited from the composite state. The E4 event does not cause the object to exit the C state and simply triggers the A_Internal action.

Source state	Event	Actions	Target state
C	E4	A_Internal	C (in A)

In the C state, the E6 event causes the object to exit the state and therefore triggers the C_Out action, then leads to the B state and, consequently, triggers the B_In action.

Source state	Event	Actions	Target state
C	E6	C_Out, B_In	B (in A)

Is the E3 event possible in the B state? Yes, as the self-transitions are inherited from the superstate. The E3 event firstly causes the object to exit the B state, and triggers the B_Out action, then causes the object to exit the A superstate and triggers A_Out, next triggers the x3 action, then causes the object to enter the A superstate and triggers A_In; it finally causes the object to re-enter the B state and triggers the B_In action.

Source state	Event	Actions	Target state
B	E3	B_Out, A_Out, x3, A_In, B_In	B (in A)

We have already examined the arrival of E5 in the B state:

Source state	Event	Actions	Target state
B	E5	B_Out, C_In	C (in A)

Watch out, there is a trap! In the C state, the E3 event firstly causes the object to exit the C state and triggers the C_Out action, then causes the object to exit the A composite state and triggers A_Out, next triggers the x3 action, then causes the object to enter the A composite state and triggers A_In, finally causes the object to re-enter the B state (as this is the initial substate!) and triggers the B_In action.

Source state	Event	Actions	Target state
C	E3	C_Out, A_Out, x3, A_In, B_In	B (in A)

In the B state, the E2 event firstly causes the object to exit the B state and triggers the B_Out action, then exits the A composite state and triggers A_Out, and finally triggers the x2 action.

Source state	Event	Actions	Target state
B	E2	B_Out, A_In, x2	...

Training request

We are going to complete the case study on training requests, which we have already dealt with from the functional (Chapter 2) and static (Chapter 4) views, by constructing the state diagram of the *TrainingRequest* class.

***   6.8   Construct the state diagram of training request.

Answer 6.8

What information have we already gathered on the dynamics of a training request? Let's go back to the first three sentences of the problem statement in Chapter 2:

1. The training process is initialised when the training manager receives a training request on behalf of an employee. This request is acknowledged by the training manager who qualifies it and then forwards his agreement or disagreement to the person who is interested.

2. In the case of agreement, the training manager looks in the catalogue of registered courses for a training course corresponding to the request. He or she informs the employee of the course content and suggests to him or her a list of subsequent sessions. When the employee sends back his or her choice, the training manager enrols the entrant in the session with the relevant training body.

3. If something crops up, the employee must inform the training manager as soon as possible to cancel the enrolment or request.

We had also constructed an activity diagram of the training process showing the main business objects and their changes in state (refer to Figure 2.12):

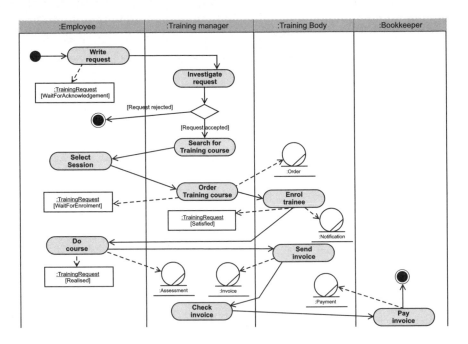

Figure 6.17   Activity diagram of the training process

From the basis of this activity diagram, we can first of all identify four main states of the training request, as illustrated on the following figure.

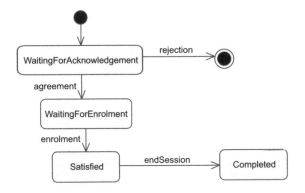

Figure 6.18   Initial state diagram of the training request

In fact, by rereading the first sentence carefully, we realise that the request is initiated by the employee and sent to the training manager, then acknowledged by the latter who forwards his agreement or disagreement to the person who is interested. In order to be able to complete the state diagram, we will first of all give details of the scenarios by using sequence diagrams.

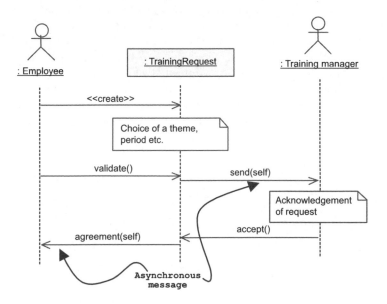

Figure 6.19   Sequence diagram illustrating the beginning of the state diagram

We will note the distinctive symbol of the asynchronous message (the half-open arrow head[42]) that is used on the preceding diagram to distinguish the actions of notification that are carried out within the context of the training request.

Control flows of messages

A synchronous control flow means that the transmitter object is frozen whilst waiting for the response from the receiver of the message.

---

42.   Notice that UML 2.0 seems to remove the difference between the flat and asynchronous messages. So this graphical distinction will probably disappear... The last proposal from UML 2.0 specifications is the following: "Asynchronous Message have an open arrow head; Synchronous Messages typically represent method calls and are shown with a filled arrow head. The reply message from a method has a dashed line; Object creation Message has a dashed line with an open arrow."

On the other hand, in an asynchronous control flow, the transmitter object does not wait for the receiver's response and continues its job without concerning itself with the receipt of its message.

This first sequence diagram leads us to add a state in front of "Waiting-ForAcknowledgement", as it is the request's validation that triggers its forwarding to the training manager. The actual creation of this request is not atomic, as the employee has to make several choices (theme, period, etc.) before proceeding with validation. We have also identified send actions that are identified as such by the send keyword on the transitions of the state diagram.

Let's continue with another sequence diagram that brings into play the "training body" actor for the normal succession of events on the training request.

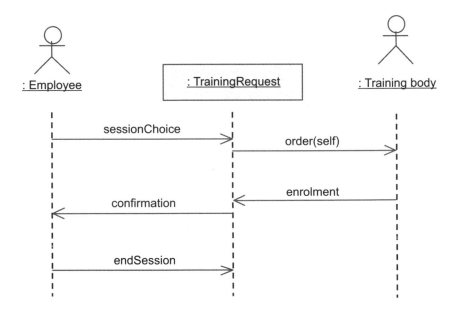

Figure 6.20 Sequence diagram illustrating the follow-up of the state diagram

We can now consolidate the information from the two sequence diagrams so as to construct a new, more complete version of the state diagram (see Figure 6.21).

What else does our state diagram need for it to be complete? All the cancellation and error transitions actually. The employee can thus cancel his or her request at any time, the training body can notify that a session is cancelled, etc.

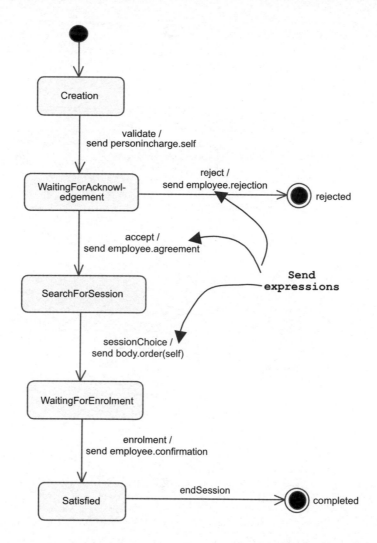

Figure 6.21 Second version of the state diagram of the training request

The complete state diagram is represented on the following figure.

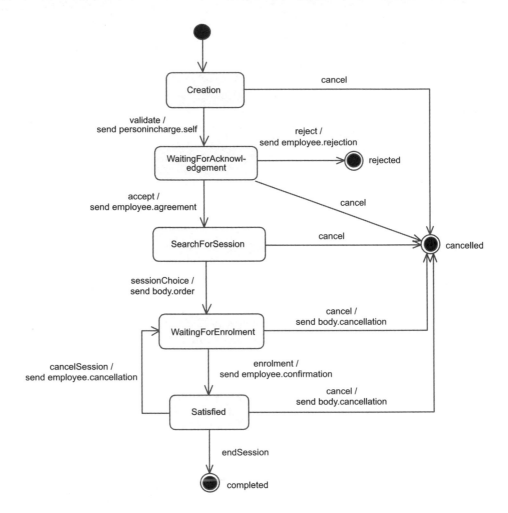

Figure 6.22   Complete state diagram of the training request

Glossary & tips

This appendix comprises a thematic glossary of the dynamic view (mainly inspired by the one found in the UML 2.0 Specifications from OMG), as well as a summary of tips which have been taken from the two previous chapters.

Glossary

Action	Fundamental unit of behaviour specification that represents some transformation of processing in the modelled system, be it a computer system or a real-world system. Actions are contained in activites, which provide thier context.
Action state	State that represents the execution of an atomic action, typically the invocation of an operation.
Activity	Specification of parameterised behaviour that is expressed as a flow of execution via a sequencing of subordinate units (whose primitive elements are individual actions).
Actor	Construct that is employed in use cases that define a role that a user or any other system plays when interacting with the system under consideration. Actors may represent human users, external hardware, or other subjects.
Completion transition	Transition without an explicit trigger event. Represents the ending of the finite activity of the source state.
Composite state	State that consists of either concurrent (orthogonal) substates or sequential (disjoint) substates.
Concurrent substate	A substate that can be held simultaneously with other substates contained in the same composite state. Contrast: *disjoint substate*
Condition (guard)	Boolean expression that must resolve to true so that the transition carrying it is validated when the trigger event occurs.

Continuous activity	An activity that only stops when an interrupting event takes place, and that makes the object exit the enclosing state.
Disjoint substate	Substate that cannot be held simultaneously with other substates contained in the same composite state. Contrast: *concurrent substate*.
Entry action	Action that is executed each time the object enters the state involved, regardless of the transition taken to reach that state, and formalised by the `entry` keyword.
Event	Specification of a significant occurence that has a location in time and space and can cause the execution of an associated behaviour. In the context of state diagrams, an event is an occurence that can trigger a transition.
Exit action	Action that is executed each time the object leaves the state involved, regardless of the transition taken to exit that state, and formalised by the `exit` keyword.
Final state	Special kind of state signifying that the enclosing composite state or the entire state machine is completed.
Finite activity	An activity that can be interrupted by an event, but in any case, which stops by itself after a certain amount of time, or when a certain condition is met.
Initial state	Special kind of state signifying the source for a single transition to the default state of the composite state.
Internal transition	Transition signifying a response to an event without changing the state of an object.
Lifeline	Modelling element that represents an individual participant in an interaction. A lifeline represents only one interacting entity.
Message	Specification of the conveyance of information from one instance to another, with the expectation that activity will ensue. A message may specify the raising of a signal or the call of an operation.
Pseudo-state	Vertex in a state machine that has the form of a state, but doesn't behave as a state. Pseudo-states include initial, final and history vertices.
Scenario	Specific sequence of actions that illustrates behaviours. A scenario may be used to illustrate an interaction or the execution of a use case instance.

Self-transition	Transition for which the target state is the same as the source state. Nevertheless it brings about an exit of state then a re-entry into this same state, which triggers the possible exit and entry actions.
Signal	Specification of an asynchronous stimulus that triggers a reaction in the receiver in an asynchronous way and without a reply. The receiving object handles the signal as specified by its receptions. The data carried by a send request and passed to it by the occurence of the send invocation event that caused the request is represented as attributes of the signal instance. A signal is defined independently of the classifiers handling the signal.
State	Condition or situation during the life of an object during which it satisfies some condition, performs some activity, or waits for some event.
State machine diagram	Diagram that depicts discrete behaviour modelled through finite state-transition systems. In particular, it specifies the sequences of states that an object or an interaction goes through during its life in response to events, together with its responses and actions.
Substate	State that is part of a composite state. See *concurrent state, disjoint state*.
Time event	Event that denotes the time elapsed since the current state was entered.
Transition	Relationship between two states indicating that an object in the first state will perform certain specified actions and enter the second state when a specified event occurs and specified conditions are satisfied. On such change of state, the transition is said to fire.
Vertex	Source or a target for a transition in a state machine. A vertex can be either a state or a pseudostate.

Tips

- To represent the dynamic context, use a *collaboration* diagram as follows:

  - the system in question is represented by an object in the centre of the diagram;

- this central object is surrounded by an instance of each actor;

- a link links the system to each of the actors;

- on each link, all the input and output messages of the system are listed, without numbering.

- For the effective construction of state diagrams:

  - firstly, represent the sequence of states that describes the nominal behaviour of an instance, with the associated transitions;

  - progressively add the transitions that correspond to "alternative" or exceptional behaviours;

  - complete the actions on the transitions and the activities in the states;

  - structure it all into substates and use advanced notation (entry, exit, etc.) if the diagram becomes too complex.

- Distinguish internal – when(condition) – and time – after(length) – events from those that result from the receipt of messages.

- Consider using the concept of composite state to factorise the many transitions triggered by the same event and leading to the same state.

- Be careful: on a transition, the action is always triggered *after* evaluation of the guard condition.

- Use automatic transitions correctly. An activity within a state can be either:

  - "Continuous": it only stops when an event occurs that exits the state;

  - "Finite": it can also be interrupted by an event, but in any case, it stops by itself after a certain amount of time, or when a certain condition is met.

  The completion transition of an activity, also known as *automatic transition*, is represented in UML without an event name or a keyword.

- Do not confuse action and activity: *actions* are associated with transitions and are atomic, which means that they cannot be interrupted with regard to the considered time scale; *activities*, on the other hand, have a specific length, can be interrupted, and are therefore associated with states.

- Watch out: an event (such as a transition and an action) is instantaneous by convention, or in any case, indivisible (atomic). It is therefore completely incorrect to test its duration! The only dynamic concepts in UML that possess the notion of duration are state and activity.

- Remember the difference between self-transition and internal transition:

  - In the case of a *self-transition*, the object leaves its source state to return to it later. This can have not inconsiderable secondary effects, such as the interruption then re-starting of an activity, the realisation of entry (`entry`) or exit (`exit`) actions of the state, etc. Moreover, if the state is broken down into substates, a self-transition inevitably returns the object to the initial substate.

  - On the other hand, the *internal transition* represents a pair (event/ action) which has no influence on the present state. The internal transition is declared within the symbol of the state.

- You must know how and when to use the `history` pseudostate: it enables a composite state to remember the last sequential substate that was active before an exiting transition. A transition towards the `history` state makes the last substate active again, instead of returning to the initial substate.

- Do not exploit entry and exit actions. Indeed, in the case of modifying the action on one of the transitions concerned, you must think of "defactorising" and of replacing the action on every other transition. An entry (or exit) action must truly be a characteristic of the state in which it is described and not just a device specific to factorisation.

- In your state diagrams, do not forget to describe the important action of sending a message to another object on firing of a transition. The syntax of this particular action is as follows: "/ `send` target.message".

- If an object realises several relatively independent behaviours, there are two ways to model this:

  - consider that it actually contains several objects, and that each of them realises one of its behaviours, and represent this using a composition relationship in a class diagram;

  - describe "concurrent regions" within the state diagram; the present state then becomes a vector of several lines, which can develop in parallel.

- Simple rules allow the definition of classes to be expanded from the basis of state diagrams:

- public operations correspond to the names of messages sent by the actors;

- private operations correspond to the names of messages sent to oneself;

- attributes correspond to the names of persistent data, manipulated in the actions or conditions.

- The concept of operation does not make sense on a human actor: we do not generally try to model him or her in a deterministic way. However, on a non-human actor, the list of operations represents its interface (in the sense of an API, for example) as it is used by the system in question. This turns out to be particularly useful for checking the interoperability of the two systems and for making sure that these operations are already available, or anticipated in the specifications.

- No state diagram if there are less than three states! Do not waste time in drawing state diagrams that only contain two states (the "on/ off" type), or indeed only one. In this case, the dynamics of the class are surely simple and likely to be understood directly. By following this rule, it appears that 10% of classes commonly require a detailed description in the form of a state diagram.

- Do not use all the subtleties of state diagrams without thinking about it first. The UML state diagram (with its derivative – the activity diagram) provides a lot of advanced features and can be very efficient, but also very complex. The reader who does not master all the details of it strongly runs the risk of not being able to keep up with you.

Part 4

Design

Case study: training request

Aims of the chapter

This chapter will allow us to illustrate the task of extending and refining models when we deal with design. To this end, we will go back to the case study of the training request system, which has already been analysed in accordance with different views in Chapters 2 (functional), 4 (static) and 6 (dynamic).

We will find out how to:

- define iterations from use case analysis;

- define the system architecture (with layers and partitions);

- define system operations and describe their contracts;

- use interaction diagrams to describe interactions between software objects and how to distribute the operations;

- use Jacobson's stereotypes to distinguish <<boundary>>, <<control>> and <<entity>> classes;

- pass decisions with regard to assigning responsibilities to the objects into the design class diagrams;

- transition from UML diagrams to Java code;

- describe the physical implementation of the application with the component and deployment diagrams.

Elements involved

- Iteration

- Layered architecture, package

- System sequence diagram

- System operation, operation contract

- Interaction diagram

- Boundary, control, and entity objects

- Object, link, visibility

- Class diagrams

- Operation, navigability, dependency

- Java code

- Component diagram

- Deployment diagram.

Case study 7 – Problem statement

Let's go back to the case study on training requests, which we have already analysed in accordance with its different views.

First of all, we will define iterations from the basis of work that has already been carried out and set ourselves as our goal the design of one of these iterations, with Java language as our target.

7.1   Step 1 – Defining iterations

In Chapter 2, we identified the use cases of the system for managing applications.

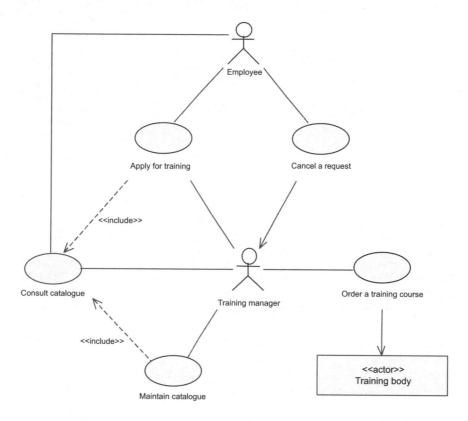

Figure 7.1   Use case diagram of the system for managing training requests

We also constructed a business model in Chapter 4. The three packages of business classes are recalled below.

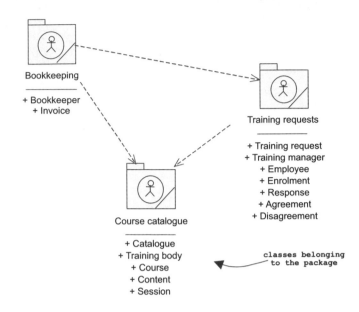

Figure 7.2 Dependencies between business packages

** 7.1 Propose a division of the project into three initial iterations on the basis of previous analysis work.

In particular, bear in mind one of the major principles of the Unified Process: use case driven...

Answer 7.1

In view of dependencies between the business packages, as well as between the use cases, it seems natural to start with management of the catalogue. The other two business packages depend on "Course catalogue", and the core use case of "Apply for training" is linked by inclusion to the "Consult catalogue" case. In the first iteration, we will therefore choose to realise the two use cases that concern the catalogue.

For the second iteration, it is essential to deal with the main use case of the system, namely "Apply for training", together with its companion, "Cancel a request".

In a third iteration, we will deal with the more administrative aspects (enrolment, etc.) with "Order a training course", as well as the strictly bookkeeping part of managing invoices.

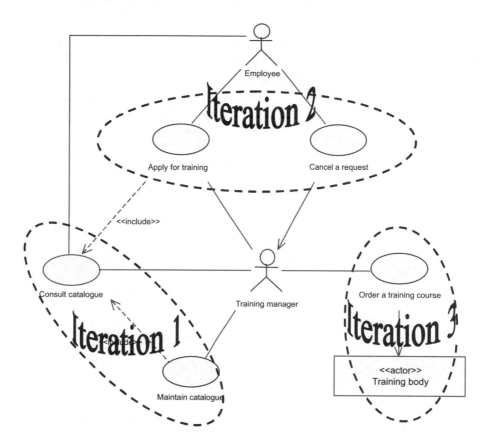

Figure 7.3 Distribution of the use cases into iterations

It is worth noting that the more technical service of authenticating the employee or training manager on the intranet can be realised in parallel to the functional use cases.

7.2 Step 2 – Defining the system architecture

Modern information systems are designed in terms of horizontal layers, which are themselves divided into vertical partitions.

The general issue of the architecture of information systems is not the topic of this book. Nevertheless, we will take advantage of this fourth section to go over a few basic ideas on the subject of layered architectures – also known as "multi-tier" – as well as the UML diagrams that are useful for this activity.

Three-tier Architecture

The three-tier architecture, now standard practice, was though as a logical division at the start, but was often wrongly interpreted as implying execution nodes that are physically distinct.

The main aim of this separation into three layers (presentation, logic, storage) is to isolate the business logic from presentation classes (GUI), as well as to forbid direct access to back-end storage layer by presentation objects. The primary concern is to respond to the criterion of flexibility: to be able to modify the interface of the application without having to modify the business rules, and to be able to change storage mechanism without having to adapt the interface or the business rules.

Below is an example of classic three-tier architecture, based on the case study of Chapter 2: the supermarket cash register.[43]

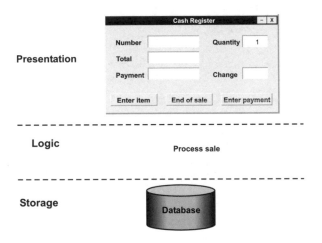

Figure 7.4 Three-tier architecture of the cash register

Nowadays, we no longer consider this division into three layers to be sufficient if we have very high goals of modularity and reuse to be met. Indeed, it can lead

---

43. The GUI is directly inspired from the one proposed by C. Larman in *Applying UML and Patterns*.

graphical presentation objects to know the detailed organisation of the logical layer, which harms their ability to be maintained and reused.

In order to improve this separation of concerns, an interesting idea consists in inserting an artificial object, often known as "controller",[44] between the graphical objects and the business objects. It is the *controller* design object that now knows the interface of objects of the business layer, and which plays the role of "façade" with regard to the presentation layer, as shown on the following figure.

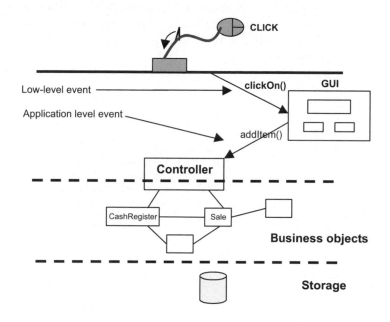

Figure 7.5 Diagram illustrating the addition of the controller object

We can now gather these controller objects, introduced in the design stage, in a new layer called "application logic", which works towards realising the use cases of the system, and isolating the presentation layer from business objects, which are often persistent and likely to be reused. The business objects will remain together in a layer called "business logic", so that the middle tier in the classical three-tier architecture is now broken down into two layers with "application logic" on top of "business logic".

We are going to apply these principles of multi-tiered architectures in the remainder of the chapter within the context of the system for managing training requests.

---

44. This is the name given by Larman in *Applying UML and Patterns* to one of his GRASP Patterns. But it refers also to the well-known "Model-View-Controller" and to Jacobson's <<control>> classes that we will explain a little further on in this chapter.

Packages, layers and partitions

In UML, the only available mechanism for organising classes into groups is the package. Consequently, horizontal layers and vertical partitions are also conveyed by packages.

So, a layered architecture is best described by a static diagram that only shows packages and their dependencies. UML 2.0 recently acknowledged the importance of this kind of high-level diagram by adding the "Package diagram" as a full-fledged kind of diagram.

You can use the predefined stereotype, « layer », to distinguish packages that represent layers.

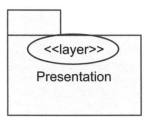

Figure 7.6   UML representation of a software layer

* * *   7.2   Propose a preliminary architecture diagram of the project on the basis of previous advice given.

Answer 7.2

We are therefore describing a package stereotyped « layer » by software layer. Within each layer, we give a preliminary structure in partitions.

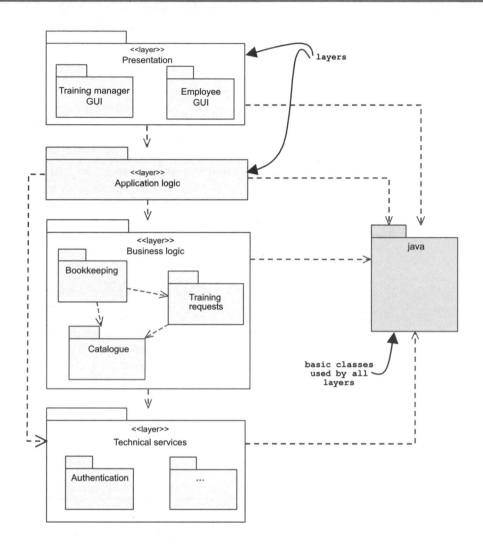

Figure 7.7 Layered architecture of the system for managing training requests

The business layer comprises *a priori* the three packages that were identified in Chapter 4: *Bookkeeping, Training requests* and *Catalogue.* We will be able to refine this division at a later stage in our study: this is only a preliminary structuring.

Details of the application layer are not given on the diagram. It can be structured either the same way as the business layer, or alternatively, from a functional view by copying the use case packages.

For the most part, the presentation layer groups the graphical classes of the respective interfaces of the training manager and of the employee.

The technical services layer consists of at least one package to manage the technical service of authentication, identified from Chapter 2 onwards. It will contain also the technical classes that provide persistency mechanisms, often known as "data access objects".

Finally, we must not forget the basic Java classes provided by the JDK and which are used by all layers. For example, the presentation layer will use graphical classes. As for the technical services layer, it will make particular use of the JDBC classes for access to relational databases. All the layers will use basic classes, such as containers, dates, etc.

However, we must consider that this preliminary architecture will be able to be refined or modified (mainly at the level of partitions within each layer) by the design task that will follow. Do not forget that the analysis/design process is inherently iterative.

7.3   Step 3 – Defining system operations (iteration 1)

Iteration 1 corresponds to the "Consult catalogue" and "Maintain catalogue" use cases. With regard to these, we carried out a high-level description in Chapter 2 (Answer 2.8). To refresh our memory, here they are again:

"The training manager can enter a new course in the catalogue, modify an existing course or take out one that a body has withdrawn. He or she can also modify groups of courses called themes. In addition, he or she can update the dates and times of the sessions.

In order to be able to apply for training and to maintain the catalogue, the system must offer a basic functionality for consulting the catalogue. This functionality can therefore be factorised in a new inclusion use case."

** 7.3   List the system operations for the "Maintain catalogue" use case.

See Chapter 2, Answer 2.5...

Answer 7.3

The system operations for the "Maintain catalogue" use case are easily deduced from its high-level description. Nevertheless, we must think about the creation and maintenance of the training bodies, which does not appear clearly in the text.

The system operations are brought together on the following diagram, where a class symbolises the system – seen as a black box – with its operations.

System
createCourse()
modifyCourse()
createTrainingBody()
modifyTrainingBody()
createTheme()
modifyTheme()
createSession()
modifySession()

Figure 7.8 System operations for the "Maintain catalogue" use case

To simplify matters, we have considered that the modification action also includes deletion, and skipped the trivial "`viewSomething()`" operations.

7.4 Step 4 – Operation contracts (iteration 1)

We identified the system operations in the previous step. But how can we specify the result of the execution of a system operation?

Operation contract

In the book we have already mentioned, Larman proposed establishing a "contract" for each system operation.

An operation contract describes changes in the state of the system when a system operation is carried out. These modifications are expressed in terms of "postconditions", which detail the new state of the system after execution of the operation.

The main postconditions concern the creation (or destruction) of objects and links descended from the analysis static model, as well as the modification of attribute values. Operation contracts thus allow the link to be made between the functional/dynamic view of use cases and the static analysis view.

A standard textual description plan for an operation contract is given below:

- name

- responsibilities

- references

- preconditions
- postconditions
- exceptions (optional)
- notes (optional)

**   7.4   Write the contract of the *createCourse* system operation.

Use the aforementioned standard plan.

Answer 7.4

First of all, we will take the part concerned with our question from the class diagram of the Catalogue package that we elaborated in Chapter 4 (cf. Figure 4.42). The *createCourse* and *createTheme* system operations are going to have an effect on the objects and links of the following diagram:

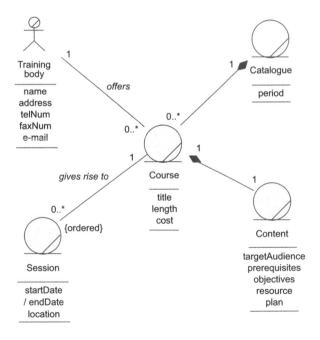

Figure 7.9   Class diagram of the Course catalogue package

However, the notion of theme was missing in our business model. This concept of theme is purely applicative: it makes the work of the employee easier when applying for a course by allowing him or her to remain deliberately imprecise and choose a set of courses on a given subject, rather than a specific course.

We will assume that the themes structure the catalogue, but that they do not divide it: a course belongs to at least one theme. The following figure shows the modifications brought about by introducing the concept of theme.

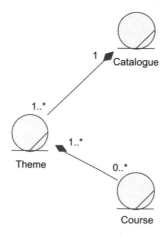

Figure 7.10 Introduction of the concept of theme

We can now describe the *createCourse* operation contract:

- **Name**
  createCourse.

- **Responsibilities**
  To create a new course according to the description provided by the training body concerned and to classify it in at least one of the existing themes.

- **References**
  Maintain catalogue use case.

- **Preconditions**

  - the course catalogue exists;

  - there is at least one theme in the catalogue;

  - the body providing the course already exists in the catalogue;

  - the training manager is connected to the intranet.

- **Postconditions**

  - a course, c1, has been created with its attributes;

  - a content object, c2, has been created with its attributes;

  - c2 has been linked to c1;

  - c1 has been linked to the providing body;

  - possible session objects have been created with their attributes;

  - these session objects have been linked with c1;

  - c1 has been linked to at least one theme.

7.5 Step 5 – Interaction diagrams (iteration 1)

Operation contracts constitute the most detailed information that can be issued with regard to analysis. Indeed, if they describe what an operation does in terms of changes in state, they should not describe how it goes about it.

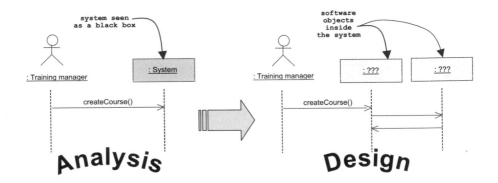

Figure 7.11 Moving from analysis to design

In fact, it is the job of the designer to choose how software objects will interact among themselves in order to realise such system operation. Jacobson[45] was the first to propose class stereotypes to describe the realisation of a use case. We will

---

45. Refer in particular to *The Unified Software Development Process*, I. Jacobson et al., Addison-Wesley, p. 44, 1999.

draw our inspiration from his work to replace the system seen as a black box (from the analysis view) with software objects (from the design view), as illustrated by the sequence diagram shown above.

Jacobson's stereotypes

Within the system, Jacobson distinguishes the following three stereotypes:

- <<boundary>>: classes that are used to model the interactions between the system and its actors;

- <<control>>: classes used to represent the coordination, sequence and control of other objects – in general, they are linked to a specific use case;

- <<entity>>: classes that are used to model long-lasted and often persistent information.

We will use these three stereotypes (with their associated graphical symbols in the interaction diagrams) to give a graphical depiction of how a message sent by an actor traverses the presentation, application logic and business logic layers.[46]

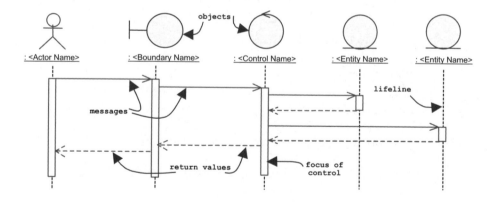

Figure 7.12 Illustration of the three Jacobson's stereotypes on a sequence diagram

46. Even though Jacobson (and then RUP from Rational) intended these stereotypes for what he calls "analysis", we prefer to use them at a "logical design" level. We will detail this logical design further according to the chosen implementation platform (J2EE, .NET, etc.) and replace for instance boundary classes with JSP (J2EE) or ASP (.NET), entity classes with EJB (J2EE), and so on.

Note the representation of the "focus of control" – white rectangles that represent periods of activity on the lifelines of objects – as well as the dashed arrows indicating return values.

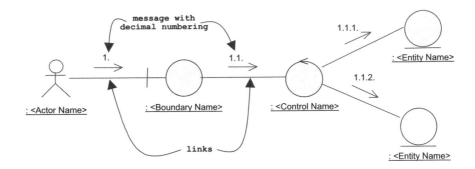

Figure 7.13 Illustration of Jacobson's three stereotypes on a collaboration diagram

Note the decimal numbering that enables nesting of messages to be shown, in a way comparable to the representation of the "focus of control" on the preceding diagram.

****   7.5   Realise a sequence diagram or a collaboration[47] diagram that demonstrates the realisation of the *createCourse* system operation.

Answer 7.5

What do we have to do? To find out, we must go back to all the postconditions listed in the preceding step:

- a course, c1, has been created with its attributes;

- a content object, c2, has been created with its attributes;

- c2 has been linked to c1;

- c1 has been linked to the providing body;

- possible session objects have been created with their attributes;

47. We have chosen to keep the well-known (obsolete!) name "collaboration diagram" throughout the book, even through UML 2.0 just renamed it "communication diagram"...

- these session objects have been linked with c1;

- c1 has been linked to at least one theme.

Do not forget that postconditions only represent the new state of the system once the system operation has been executed. They are certainly not ordered: it is the role of the designer to choose now which object must realise each action, and in which order.

The core postcondition concerns the creation of the course object, with its content and its sessions, then the definition of its links with the other objects of the catalogue, such as the themes and bodies. It seems reasonable to think that the creation of the course object – c1 – will be done in four steps.

1. initialisation of c1 object and of its attributes,

2. creation of its content,

3. creation of sessions,

4. validation of c1.

By examining it in detail, let's find a possible solution for the first step, involving two « boundary » objects, a « control » one and an « entity » one.

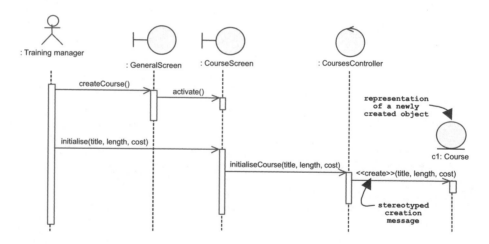

Figure 7.14 Sequence diagram of the initialisation of c1

The same scenario can be represented by a collaboration diagram, such as the one shown on Figure 7.15:

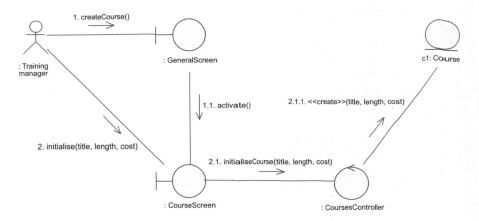

Figure 7.15 Collaboration diagram of the initialisation of c1

Let's continue with the creation of the content. The completed sequence diagram then becomes:

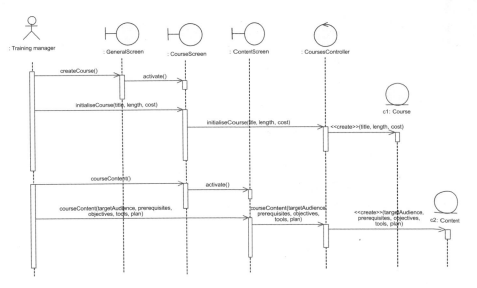

Figure 7.16 Sequence diagram of the initialisation of c1 and of the creation of its content

We will observe that the sequence diagram is becoming increasingly difficult to read as we add objects... It is for this simple reason that the collaboration diagram is essential for design: it allows us to place our objects in both dimensions, thereby improving the readability of the diagram.

The collaboration diagram that corresponds to the preceding sequence diagram is given on the following figure by way of comparison. From now on, we will exclusively use the collaboration diagram.

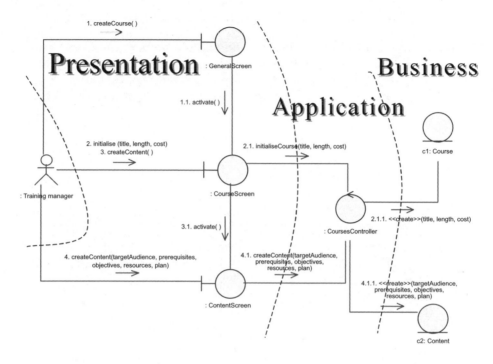

Figure 7.17 Collaboration diagram of the initialisation of c1 and of the creation of its content

Note that the collaboration diagram above is set out in such a way that it is easy for the reader to differentiate the object layers.

Let's now carry on with the creation of the sessions.

Multiobjects

In order to indicate that the course, c1, will be linked to a collection of sessions, we use a *multiobject*. The *multiobject* is a UML construction that represents several objects of the same class in a single symbol. This prevents detailed design classes linked to the programming language (such as *Vector* of the C++ STL or *ArrayList* in Java, etc.) from being added too soon. A multiobject can also represent the complete abstraction of a connection with a database.

Moreover, we had forgotten to create this empty collection in Figure 7.16 when creating c1. After the creation of each session, all you have to do is add it to the collection. For this, we use a generic operation, *add()*: see Figure 7.18.

The collaboration diagram possesses another advantage over the sequence diagram: it allows the representation of structural relationships among objects. For example, we have made the composition links appear around the course object, c1, in order to make it easier when we construct our future design class diagram.

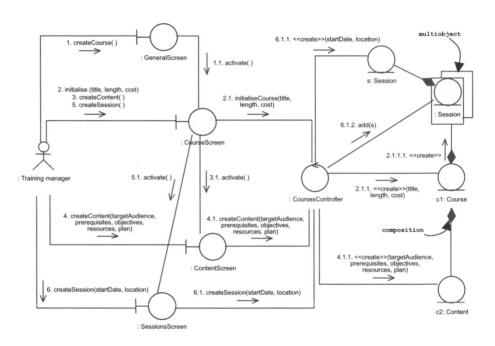

Figure 7.18 Collaboration diagram of the initialisation of c1, of the creation of its content and of a session

All we have to do now is link the course, c1, to an existing theme and validate the creation. By comparing the task realised in the postconditions, which were required at the start of the answer, we can state that the following has not been taken into account: "c1 has been linked to the providing body". We simply add it to the responsibilities of the controller when creating the course.

The complete collaboration diagram of the *createCourse* system operation can be found on the following figure (7.19). Observe the quantity of information – quite considerable – that manages to be represented in, yet again, a barely legible way on a single page. Nevertheless, we are already reaching the limits of the collaboration diagram (and we have long since exceeded those of the sequence diagram!).

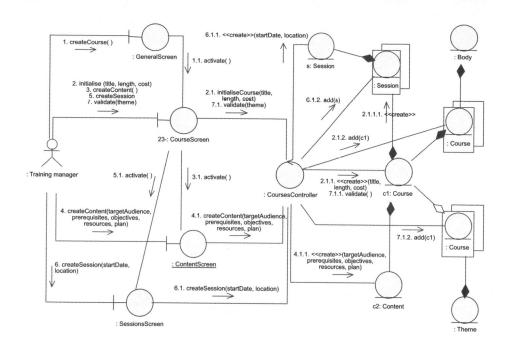

Figure 7.19 Complete collaboration diagram of the *createCourse* system operation

An interesting idea for improving the readability of the diagram entails dividing it into two by treating the controller object as a transition marker:

- one part to specify the dynamics of the human-computer interface with the actors, the <<boundary>> objects and the <<control>> object;

- a second part to specify the dynamics of the application and business layers with the <<control>> object and the <<entity>> objects.

The resulting partial collaboration diagrams are shown on the following two figures.

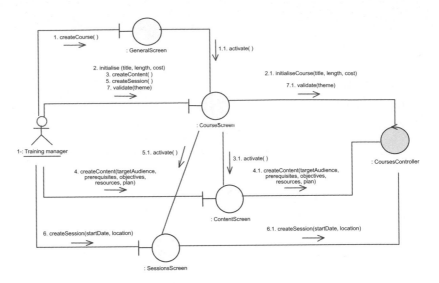

Figure 7.20 Partial collaboration diagram of the *createCourse* system operation: presentation layer and link with the application layer

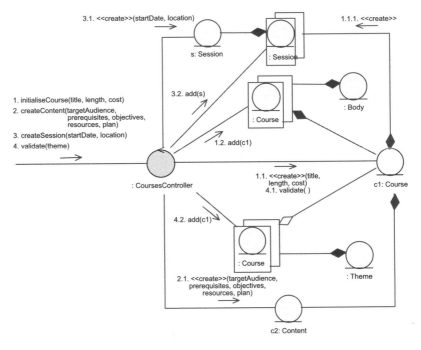

Figure 7.21 Partial collaboration diagram of the *createCourse* system operation: application layer and link with the business layer

7.6 Step 6 – Design class diagrams (iteration 1)

Each system operation will in turn give rise to a dynamic study in the form of a collaboration diagram, as was the case for the *createCourse* operation in Answer 7.5.

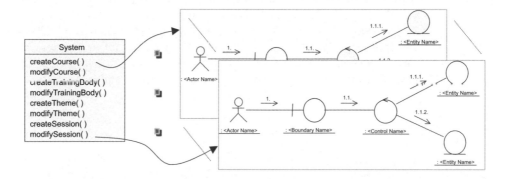

Figure 7.22 Design process initialised by the system operations

The collaboration diagrams that are thus realised will enable development of design class diagrams, and this is done by adding mainly the following information to classes from the analysis model:

- operations: a message can only be received by an object if its class has declared the corresponding public operation;

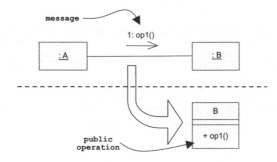

Figure 7.23 Relationship between message and operation

- the navigability of associations or the dependencies between classes, according to whether the links between objects are long-lasted or temporary, and according to the direction in which messages are circulating.

Long-lasted or temporary links

A long-lasted link between objects will give rise to a navigable association between the corresponding classes; a temporary link (by parameter: « parameter », or local variable: « local ») will give rise to a dependency relationship.

On the example presented below, the link between object :A and object :B becomes a navigable association between the corresponding classes. The fact that object :A receives a reference passed as parameter from a message on an object of class C results in a dependency between the classes concerned.

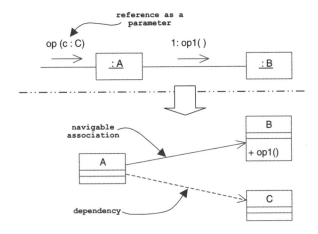

Figure 7.24 Traceability from links between objects to relationships between classes

Finally, note that we recommend that you do not add the classes, which correspond to multiobjects in the design class diagram. This enables our "logical" design to remain independent from the target programming language for as long as possible.

***   7.6   By applying the rules set out above, construct a design class diagram fragment from the partial collaboration diagram, Figure 7.21 (*createCourse*).

Answer 7.6

The collaboration diagram of Figure 7.21 first of all allows us to add operations in the classes, as shown on the following diagram.

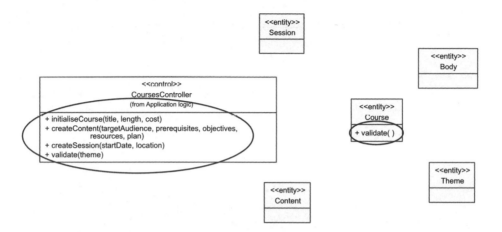

Figure 7.25 Operations in the design classes

Note that there are very few operations, as we are withholding the following:

- Creation operations (<<create>> message),

- Generic operations on the container classes (*add*( ), etc.).

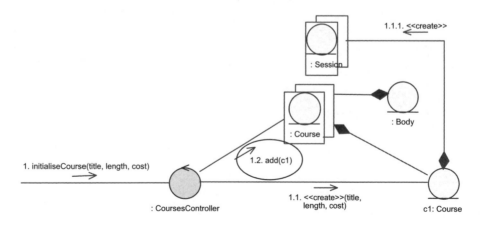

Figure 7.26 Collaboration diagram restricted to the first message of the *createCourse* system operation

Nevertheless, we can spot a first problem: how can the *coursesController* object add the new course, c1, to the multiobject of the corresponding Body without possessing a reference on this Body?

This means that we have to add a parameter to the *initialiseCourse* operation: a reference towards an existing Body.

If we also use stereotypes to indicate temporary links between objects, the preceding collaboration diagram is altered as follows:

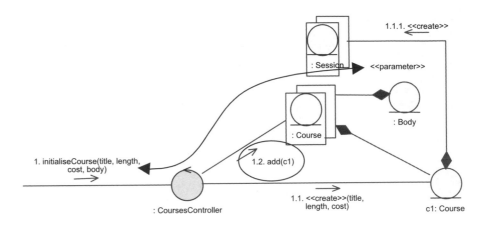

Figure 7.27   Completed collaboration diagram

We will now complete the class diagram by adding the relationships between classes: association (with its variants of aggregation or composition) and dependency. The task is made easier in that we had already indicated the composition and aggregation links on the collaboration diagram.

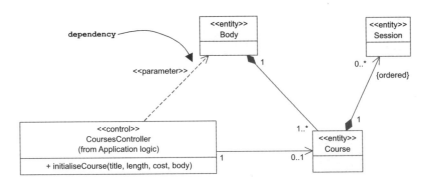

Figure 7.28   Class diagram realised in accordance with the preceding collaboration diagram

Note the use of the predefined stereotype, « parameter »[48] on the dependency between the *CoursesController* and *Body* classes, which is there to mirror the type of temporary link that exists between the corresponding objects in the collaboration diagram.

If we now apply the same process to the whole of Figure 7.21, we obtain the design class diagram below. It is important to be aware of the fact that we have made the attributes appear in the classes, but not the parameters of the operations (in order to simplify the diagram).

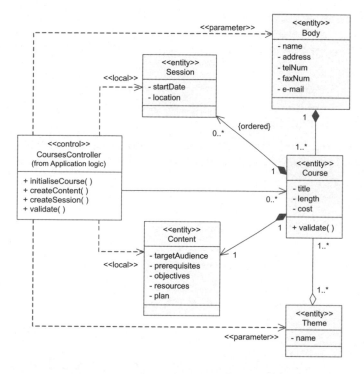

Figure 7.29 Completed design class diagram

Of course, this diagram is still at a provisional stage:

- the choices for navigability of the associations are far from conclusive – we will be able to verify them through studying other system operations;

- the dependencies will perhaps be converted into associations if the objects call for a durable link, and not a simple temporary link, within the context of other system operations.

---

48. This is no longer a predefined stereotype in UML 2.0 (neither « local »)... But you can use this interesting adornment.

****   7.7   From the basis of the diagrams realised during the preceding question, propose improvements for the object-oriented design that they illustrate.

Answer 7.7

The class diagram in Figure 7.29 presents a *CoursesController* class that is coupled to all the other classes! This property is completely contrary to a basic principle of object-oriented design, commonly called "low coupling".[49]

Low coupling

"Coupling" represents a measure of the quantity of other classes, to which a given class is connected, which it knows about and on which it depends.

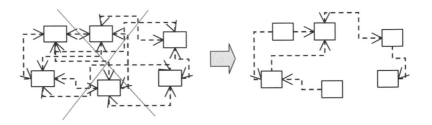

Figure 7.30   Coupling between classes

Low coupling is a principle that you must keep in mind for all design decisions; it is an underlying objective, which is to be assessed continuously. If we apply this pattern while evaluating all design choices, we generally obtain a more flexible design that is easier to maintain.

The notion of "controller" object, which we explained in detail previously (cf. Figure 7.5) is a good example of means used to minimise coupling between software layers.

Let's try to see if there is a simple means for reducing coupling of the *CoursesController* class without increasing that of the other classes as a consequence.

---

49.   [Larman 97] pp.200–202.

Let's go back to the collaboration diagram in Figure 7.21. Is the *CoursesController* object really in the best position to create the *Content* and *Session* objects? Instead, could it not delegate this responsibility of creation to the *Course* object which, in any case, is then going to be linked durably to its content and its sessions? In this way, we are removing the two dependencies between *CoursesController* and *Content* and *Session*, without adding any, as *Course* is already interfaced to *Content* and *Session* by strong composition relationships.

The collaboration diagram can therefore be altered as demonstrated on the following figure.

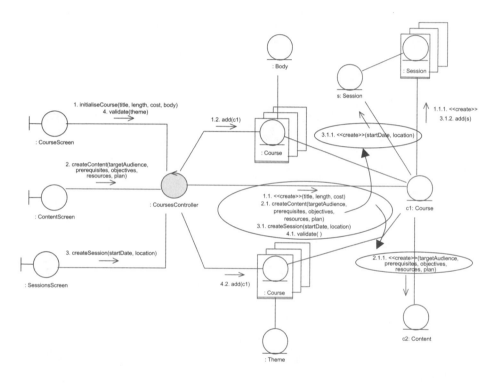

Figure 7.31 Improved collaboration diagram of the *createCourse* system operation

The design class diagram is thus relieved of two dependencies, simply because the *CoursesController* object knew how to delegate part of its responsibilities to the *Course* object. In fact, this simple example is completely representative of the iterative work of evaluation and improvement that every designer must do as regards object-oriented design.

To finish, we will complete the improved class diagram by the types of attributes, and carry out the complete signature of the operations (parameters with their type). It is important to note that we are using simple types from Java language (such as *int* and *short*), basic Java classes (such as *String* and *Date*), user "primitive" classes (such as *Number* and *Email*), which we will have to define precisely – and finally, classes from the model (such as *Theme* and *Body*).

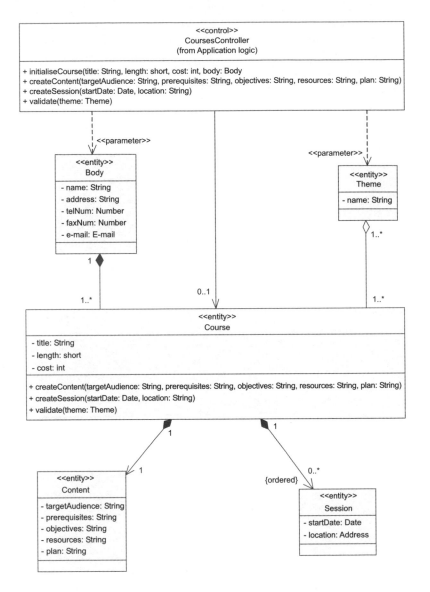

Figure 7.32 Improved design class diagram

7.7   Step 7 – Defining the system operations (iteration 2)

At this stage, we are taking it as agreed that iteration 1 has been realised successfully. The "Consult catalogue" and "Maintain catalogue" use cases have been designed, implemented and tested. The "Course catalogue" business package has been refined, and as a result, expanded. A possible state of its design class diagram (only showing the <<entity>> classes) is presented on the following figure.

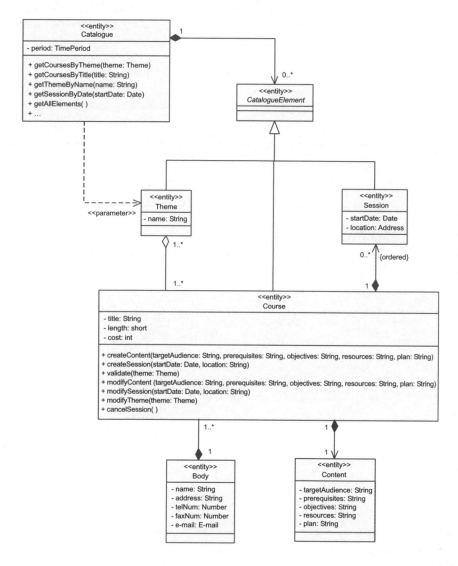

Figure 7.33   Design class diagram of the Catalogue package

Note that many operations have been added, as well as an abstract class, *CatalogueElement*, which includes the themes, courses and sessions in the light of an employee creating a training request from the basis of any element of the course catalogue.

We assume that storing the catalogue in a relational database is in operation, as well as the graphical user interface of the two use cases.

We are now going to design and implement the second iteration. Let's begin with the *Apply for training* use case. Its high-level description was realised in Chapter 2 (Answer 2.8). To refresh our memory, here it is again:

"The employee can consult the catalogue and select a theme, or course, or even a specific session. The training request is automatically registered by the system and forwarded by e-mail to the training manager. If the employee has not chosen a session, but simply a course or a theme, the training manager will consult the catalogue and select the sessions that appear to correspond most to the training request. This selection will be forwarded by e-mail to the employee, who will then be able to submit a new, more specific training request."

*   7.8   List the system operations for the "Apply for training" use case.

Answer 7.8

First of all, we will construct a system sequence diagram of the main success scenario.

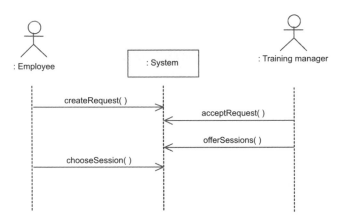

Figure 7.34 System sequence diagram of the main success scenario

It is easy to find the other system operations:

- *rejectRequest()* by the training manager,

- *cancelRequest()* by the employee.

However, be careful as the *consultCatalogue* or *orderCourse* system operations belong to other use cases.

The system operations for the *Apply for training* use case are therefore brought together on the following diagram.

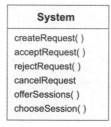

Figure 7.35 System operations for the "Apply for training" use case

7.8 Step 8 – Operation contracts (iteration 2)

Let's recall the standard textual description plan for an operation contract that was suggested previously:

- name

- responsibilities

- references

- preconditions

- postconditions

- exceptions (optional)

- notes (optional)

**

7.9   Write the contracts of the *createRequest* and *rejectRequest* system operations.

Use the preceding standard plan.

Answer 7.9

Firstly, we will take out the part concerned with our question from the class diagram of the "Training requests" package (cf. Figure 4.41). The *createRequest* and *rejectRequest* system operations will influence objects and links from the following diagram.

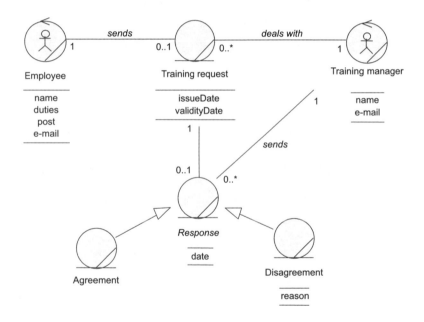

Figure 7.36   Extract of the business modelling class diagram

First of all, let's establish the contract of the *createRequest* operation:

- **Name**
  createRequest.

- **Responsibilities**
  Create an initial training request in accordance with the elements of the catalogue and forward it to the training manager for acknowledgement.

- **References**
  Apply for training use case.

- **Preconditions**

  - the course catalogue exists;

  - the employee is connected to the intranet;

  - an object, e, representing the employee exists in the application.

- **Postconditions**

  - a training request, tr, has been created;

  - the *validityDate* and *issueDate* attributes of tr have been initialised;

  - tr has been linked to the employee, e;

  - tr has been linked to an element of the course catalogue (this is an aspect that was missing in the business modelling diagram);

  - an e-mail containing tr has been forwarded to the training manager.

- **Exceptions**

  - The employee can cancel his or her training request creation at any moment before validating.

Let's continue with the contract of the *rejectRequest* operation:

- **Name**
  rejectRequest.

- **Responsibilities**
  Decline a training request forwarded by an employee and send back the reason for its rejection.

- **References**
  Apply for training use case.

- **Preconditions**

  - a training request, tr, exists;

- the training manager is connected to the intranet;

- an object, e, representing the employee exists in the application and is linked to tr.

- **Postconditions**

  - the training request, tr, has been destroyed;

  - a Disagreement object, d, has been created;

  - the date and reason attributes of d have been initialised;

  - an e-mail containing d has been forwarded to the employee, e.

- **Exceptions**
  None.

7.9   Step 9 – Interaction diagrams (iteration 2)

As in step 5 for iteration 1, we will continue our design work by constructing a collaboration diagram.

** 7.10 Construct a collaboration diagram that shows the realisation of the *createRequest* system operation.

Answer 7.10

The process is similar to that which we adopted for Answer 7.5.

The collaboration diagram representing initialisation of the training request by the employee bears a striking resemblance to that of Figure 7.15.

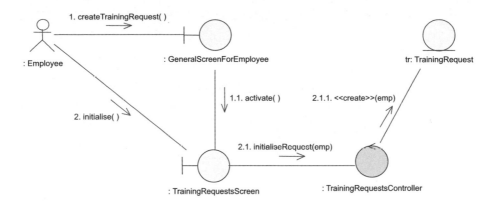

Figure 7.37   Collaboration diagram of initialisation of "tr"

Let's continue by establishing the link with an element of the training catalogue, then by positioning the *validityDate* and *issueDate* attributes, and finally by sending the message to the training manager.

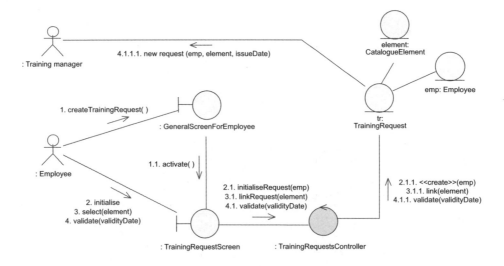

Figure 7.38   Complete collaboration diagram of the *createRequest* system operation

7.10 Step 10 – Design class diagrams (iteration 2)

* * *   7.11 Construct a design class diagram of the "Training requests" package on the model of Figure 7.33 and by extrapolating from the preceding response, as well as by relying on your knowledge of the subject.

You can also refer to the state diagram from Question 6.8.

Answer 7.11

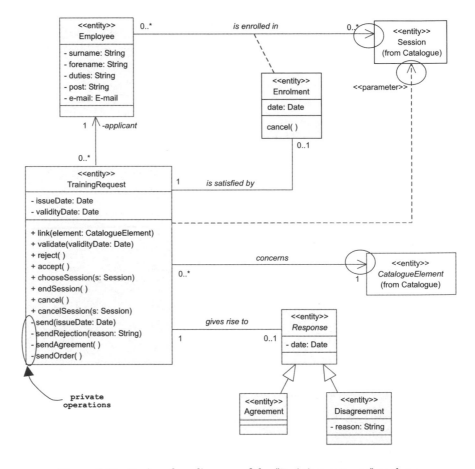

Figure 7.39 Design class diagram of the "Training requests" package

We have already covered the finer points of the class diagram in Chapters 3 and 4. The *Enrolment* association class will therefore not surprise you. Be aware of the way in which we have completed the operations compartment of the *TrainingRequest* class, particularly with the private operations, which are necessary for sending messages to actors.

We will also make a point of noting that we have shown the *Session* and *CatalogueElement* classes in the diagram, even though they do not belong to the current package. It is important to show their relationships with classes of the *Training requests* package to justify the direction of dependencies between the enclosing packages. In fact, we should only represent the navigable associations, the dependencies or generalisations, which point at classes that are external to those of the package concerned.

7.11 Step 11 – Back to architecture

** 7.12 Go back to Figure 7.7, which represented the layered architecture of the system, and display all the classes that we have identified within corresponding packages.

Do not take the technical services layer into account, nor the basic Java classes.

Answer 7.12

Just make a list of all the classes, which we have used in our various diagrams, and represent them within the appropriate package.

The detailed logical architecture of the first three layers is shown on the following figure.

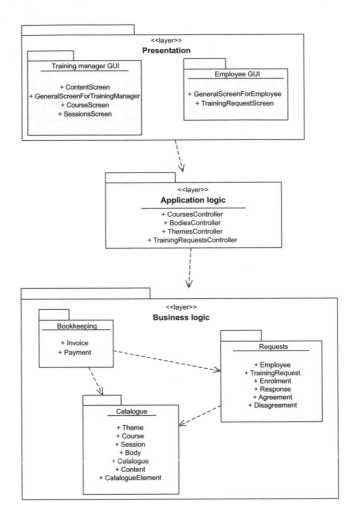

Figure 7.40 Detailed layered architecture of the first two iterations

7.12 Step 12 – Transition to Java code

The design models that we have realised enable the simple production of code in an object-oriented programming language, such as Java:

- Class diagrams enable the description of the skeleton code, i.e. all the declarations.

Production of the skeleton code from class diagrams

Our first approach:

- the UML class becomes a Java class

- UML attributes become Java instance variables

- UML operations become Java methods.

Note that the navigable roles also produce instance variables – just like the attributes – but with a user type instead of a simple type. A good tip is to use the role on the association as the instance name. The default constructor is implicit.

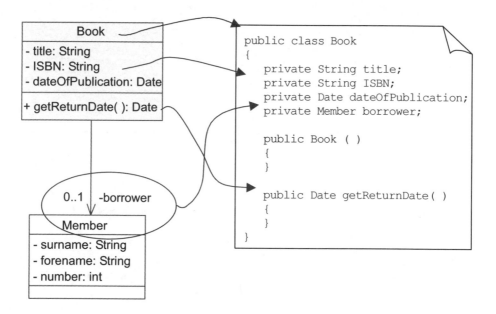

Figure 7.41 Java skeleton code of the Book class

- With the help of interaction diagrams, it is easier to write the body of methods, particularly the sequence of method calls on the objects that collaborate.

Production of the body of methods from the basis of interaction diagrams

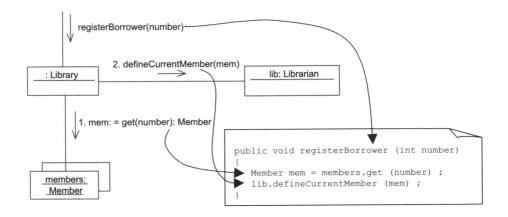

Figure 7.42 Body of the method, *registerBorrower*

** 7.13 By referring back to Figure 7.39, propose a Java skeleton code for the *TrainingRequest* class.

Answer 7.13

Let's go back to Figure 7.39, taking out what does not concern the *TrainingRequest* class. The preceding rules are sufficient for producing the skeleton of the class in Java. The only difficulty stems from the fact that we must not forget import statements for relationships with classes that belong to other packages, as well as for basic Java classes.

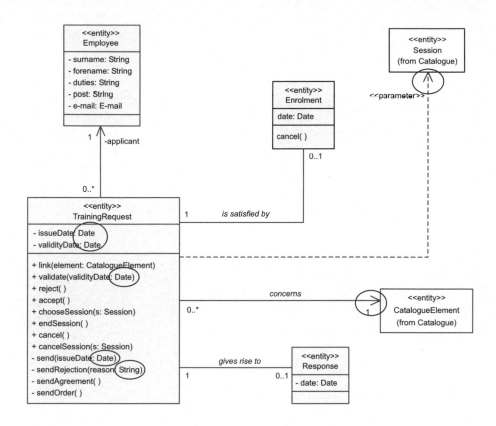

Figure 7.43 The TrainingRequest class and its relationships

The corresponding Java code is shown on the following diagram.

Notice the `import` statements, as well as the last four methods that allow read (*get*) and write (*set*) access to attributes in order to respect the principle of encapsulation (in the common style of JavaBeans).

```
package requests;

import java.user.*;
import catalogue.Session;
import catalogue.CatalogueElement;

public class TrainingRequest
{
    private Date issueDate;
    private Date validityDate;
    private Employee applicant;
    private Enrolment enrolment;
    private CatalogueElement catalogueElement;
    private Response response;

    public TrainingRequest( )
    {
    }

    public void link (CatalogueElement element)
    {
    }

    public void validate (Date validityDate)
    {
    }

    public void reject ( )
    {
    }

    public void accept ( )
    {
    }

    public void chooseSession (Session s)
    {
    }

    public void endSession ( )
    {
    }
```

```
    public void cancel ( )
    {
    }

    public void cancelSession (Session s)
    {
    }

    private void send (Date issueDate)
    {
    }

    private void sendRejection (String reason)
    {
    }

    private void sendAgreement ( )
    {
    }

    private void sendOrder ( )
    {
    }

    public Date getIssueDate ( )
    {
        return issueDate;
    }

    public void setIssueDate (Date id)
    {
        issueDate = id;
    }

    public Date getValidityDate ( )
    {
        return validityDate;
    }

    public void setValidityDate (Date vd)
    {
        validityDate = vd;
    }
}
```

Figure 7.44 Java skeleton code of the *TrainingRequest* class

*** 7.14 Refer to Figure 7.33 and propose a Java skeleton code for the *Course* class.

Answer 7.14

Let's go back to Figure 7.33, taking out what does not concern the *Course* class. A few additional difficulties crop up with regard to the preceding question:

- the generalisation relationship with *CatalogueElement*,

- the multiplicities, "1..*" with *Theme* and "0..* {ordered}" with Session.

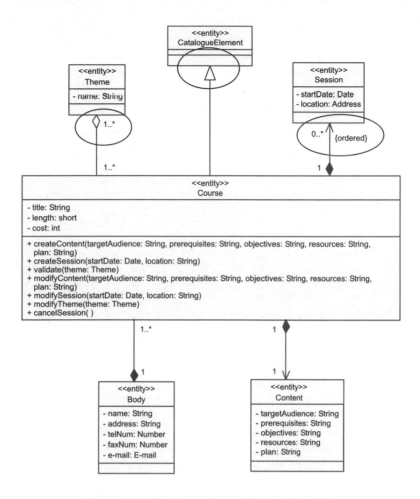

Figure 7.45 The *Course* class with its relationships

The previous rules are no longer sufficient. We have seen a conversion example of a navigable association of multiplicity "1" (or "0..1"), but how do we convey the navigable associations of multiplicity "*"?

Translating associations with multiplicity "*" in Java

The principle of it is relatively simple: a multiplicity "*" will be implemented by a reference attribute pointing to a collection instance, which contains in turn instances of the many-side class.

The difficulty consists in choosing the right collection among the many basic classes that Java offers. Although it is possible to create object arrays in Java, this is not necessarily the right solution. On this subject, we prefer instead to resort to collections, among which the ones that are used most often are *ArrayList* (formerly *Vector*) and *HashMap* (formerly *HashTable*). Use *ArrayList* if you have to respect a specific order and retrieve objects from an integer index; use *HashMap* if you wish to retrieve objects from an arbitrary key.

Here are some examples of solutions to remember so that you make a sensible choice:

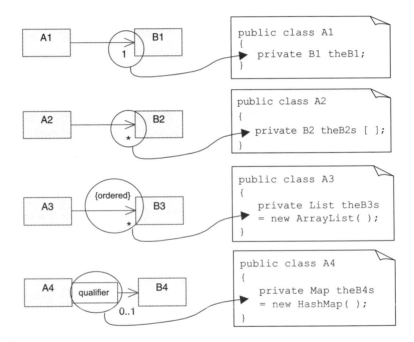

Figure 7.46   Possible ways of translating associations in Java

For the *Course* class, we will use:

• an *ArrayList* for the ordered association with the Session class,

• a *HashMap* for the association with the *Theme* class, rather than a simple array: we will use the theme name as a qualifier.

All these explanations lead us to produce the following code for the *Course* class.

```
package catalogue;

import java.util.*;

public class Course extends CatalogueElement
{
    private String title;
    private short length;
    private int cost;
    private List sessions = new ArrayList();
    private Map themes = new HashMap();
    private Content content;
    private Body body;

    public Course ( )
    {
    }

    public.void createContent (String targetAudience, String prerequisites,
        String objectives, String resources, String plan)
    {
    }

    public void createSession (Date startDate, String location)
    {
    }

    public void validate (Theme theme)
    {
    }

    public void modifyContent (String targetAudience, String prerequisites,
        String objectives, String resources, String plan)
    {
    }

    public void modifySession (Date startDate, String location)
    {
    }

    public void modifyTheme (Theme theme)
    {
    }

    public void cancelSession ( )
    {
    }

    public String getTitle ( ) {return title;}

    public void setTitle ( String t) {title = t;}

    public short getLength ( ) {return length;}

    public void setLength (short l) {length = l}

    public int getCost ( ) {return cost;}

    public void setCost (int c) {cost = c;}
;
```

Figure 7.47   Java skeleton code of the *Course* class

7.13 Step 13 – Putting the application into action

We will now describe the physical implementation of our application for managing training requests with the help of two final types of diagram offered by UML:

- the component diagram,

- the deployment diagram.

Component diagram

The component diagram shows dependencies among the software components that constitute the training request. A component can be an executable, source code, binary code, etc. In fact, a component represents every physical and replaceable part of a system that conforms to, and provides, the realisation of a set of interfaces.

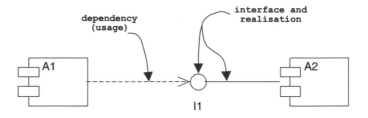

Figure 7.48   Example of components, interfaces and dependencies

***   7.15 Propose a realistic component diagram for the first two iterations of the system for managing training requests.

Only show components that are sufficiently important, which represent a collaboration between many classes.

Do not forget that the target language is Java.

Answer 7.15

The main components are deduced from all of the preceding study. Each actor has its own human-computer interface, embodied by a Java applet. These two applets use an identical, general authentication service. On the other hand, the two applets do not have the same means of access on the *Catalogue* module. We have represented the latter using the concept of interface. Indeed, the *Catalogue* module offers two different interfaces (*ITrainingManager* and *IEmployee*), enabling in particular the restriction of access to employees, who are only allowed to consult the catalogue; whereas the training manager can modify the catalogue. The catalogue is stored in a specific database, as are the employees. Finally, a reusable component, *Calendar*, is used both for the catalogue and for the training requests.

To make the diagram more complete and easier to read, we will also note that we have used a particular graphical representation for the component of database stereotype, and that we have shown the actors on the diagram.

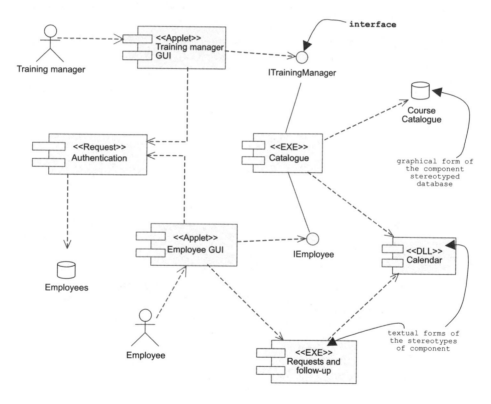

Figure 7.49 Component diagram of the first two iterations

Let's complete this case study with the deployment diagram.

Deployment diagram

The deployment diagram shows the physical configuration of different run-time processing elements that take part in executing the system, as well as the component instances that they support.

This diagram is formed from "nodes" connected by physical links. The symbols of nodes may contain component instances, as well as objects. Components that no longer exist at "run-time" do not appear on this diagram; these must be shown on component diagrams.

7.16 Propose a realistic deployment diagram for the first two iterations of the system for managing training requests.

In order to 'trim' the diagram somewhat, omit the dependencies among components.

Answer 7.16

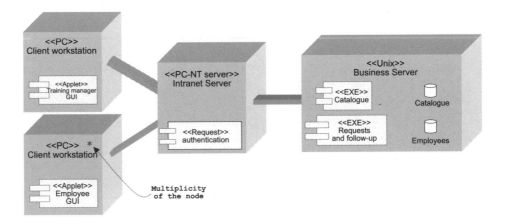

Figure 7.50 Deployment diagram of the first two iterations

Every actor has his or her own client workstation that is a PC connected to the intranet server of the organisation, which is itself a PC NT server. In particular, this intranet server contains the authentication application. As we work through this, we will notice the representation of the multiplicity of the employee's client workstation.

As regards the business server, it hosts the other applications as well as the databases. This entails a Unix machine, and this is for historical reasons...

We have therefore finished this first guided tour of the wonderful world of object-oriented design! We could touch on many more subjects: design of human-computer interfaces, management of persistence, distribution of components – to mention just a few. If you wish to go into some of these themes more deeply, then refer to the bibliography that is presented on the following page. In particular, we advise you to spend time studying the famous "Design Patterns".

Bibliography

[Ahmed 02]   *Developing Enterprise Java Application With J2EE and UML*,
K. Ahmed, C. Umrysh, Addison-Wesley, 2002.

[Coad 99]   *Java Modelling in Color With UML: Enterprise Components and Process*,
P. Coad, Prentice Hall, 1999.

[Gamma 95]   *Design Patterns: Elements of Reuseable Object-Oriented Software*,
E. Gamma et al., Addison-Wesley, 1995.

[Grand 01]   *Patterns in Java, Vol. 1* (2nd Edition), M. Grand, Wiley, 2001.

[Havdal 02]   *Java the UML Way: Integrated Object-Oriented Design and
Programming*, V. Havdal, E. Lervik, Wiley, 2002.

[Larman 01]   *Applying UML and Patterns: An Introduction to Object-Oriented
Analysis and Design* (2nd Edition), C. Larman, Prentice Hall, 2001.

[Lee 02]   *Practical Object-Oriented Development with UML and Java*, R. Lee,
W. Tepfenhart, Prentice Hall, 2002.

Complementary exercises

Aims of the chapter

By working through one last case study, this chapter will allow us to complete our spectrum of UML modelling techniques, which have been implemented during the activity of design, in particular:

- Interaction diagrams

- Design class diagrams.

Case study 8 – Problem statement

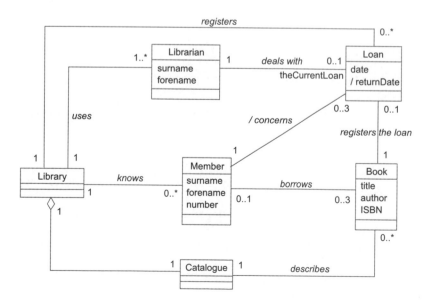

Figure 8.1 Analysis class diagram of the IS of the library

We will work from the basis of an analysis model of an information system, whose purpose is to manage a library. This library only lends books at first.

The analysis class diagram is shown on the Figure 8.1.

The provisional use case diagram is presented below.

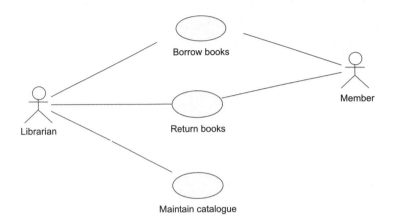

Figure 8.2   Preliminary use case diagram of the IS of the library

Let's continue with the system operations of the *Borrow books* use case, which are shown in detail on the following system sequence diagram.

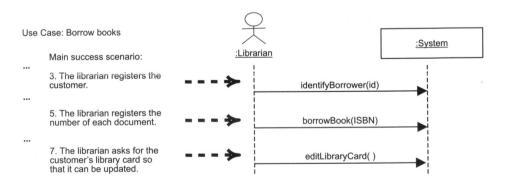

Figure 8.3   System operations of the *Borrow books* use case

We are now going to concern ourselves with the contract of the *borrowBook* operation. Note that we are passing over the first operation, *identifyBorrower*, but only because it is not as interesting as the second and would not actually contribute anything significant to our study. In reality, system operations must, of course, be viewed in chronological order.

- **Name**
  borrowBook (ISBN).

- **Responsibilities**
  Register the loan of a book, which is identified by its ISBN number.

- **References**
  Borrow books use case.

- **Preconditions**

  - the catalogue of books exists and is not empty;

  - the system has recognised the member of the library.

- **Postconditions**

  - a loan l has been created;

  - the *date* attribute of l has been set to the current date;

  - the *returnDate* attribute of l has been set to (the current date + two weeks);

  - l has been linked to book b, whose ISBN attribute equals the ISBN passed as parameter;

  - l has been linked to the member concerned and to the library.

*** 8.1 Develop a collaboration diagram for the *borrowBook* system operation using the preceding information.

Detail each of your design decisions.

Do not concern yourself with interface classes (<<boundary>>).

Answer 8.1

Our collaboration diagram starts off with receipt of a system message, which has come from an actor. As we do not have to concern ourselves with interface objects, we will go straight for an object that will process this system event.

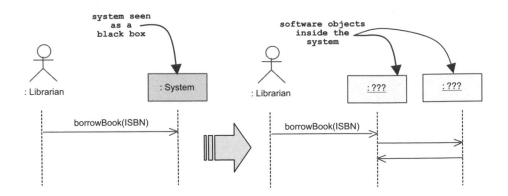

Figure 8.4 Transition from analysis to design

The solution that we implemented in the preceding chapter (step 5) led us to introduce an artificial design object of "controller" type, which we could have called *LoansController* here.

In fact, a more simple approach is possible in the case of systems comprising a restricted number of system operations, which does not enforce the addition of a new class. This solution entails using an object of an existing analysis class as a controller:

• either an object representing the whole system or the organisation itself,

• or an object representing a role that would have realised the system operation.

The first possible choice is the most straightforward one, but its major disadvantage is that we assign processing of all the system operations to a single object, which rapidly runs the risk of being overloaded as far as responsibilities are concerned. This is an acceptable solution in our example; the candidate class is the *Library* class.

In general, the second possibility enables distribution of system operations among several objects. But here, the only candidate class is the *Librarian* class, which does not contribute anything in comparison with the preceding solution. We will therefore keep *Library* as the controller object for our system operation. So, the collaboration diagram can start off in the following way.

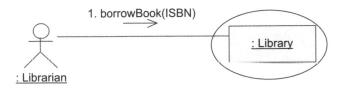

Figure 8.5 Collaboration diagram of the *borrowBook* operation (beginning)

How do we now have to proceed? We must simply study the operation contract. However, remember that the postconditions listed in the contract are not necessarily in any particular order. In our case, it nevertheless seems sensible to start by creating the loan object, as the other postconditions apply to its attributes or its links.

So, the question which must be considered is as follows: which object must be responsible for the creation of loan l?

If we go back to the analysis class diagram, we notice that four classes already possess an association with the *Loan* class; namely, *Librarian*, *Library*, *Book* and *Member*. They are therefore all good initial candidates. However, the best choice is generally provided by the class that possesses an association of composition, aggregation or "register" type. In our example, the *Library* class is rightly linked to *Loan* by a "register" association. Moreover, as the *Library* is already the controller, it constitutes the ideal candidate.

The collaboration diagram then becomes:

Figure 8.6 Collaboration diagram of the *borrowBook* operation (continuation)

At first sight, we will note the bewildering use of the <<create>> stereotyped message. Indeed, strictly speaking, the object l cannot receive the <<create>> message, as it does not exist yet! This concerns a convention offered by UML, which avoids entering considerations that depend on the target programming language. In Java (or in C++), this message for creation will probably be conveyed by the new keyword and the call of the constructor from the *Loan* class, which will return a reference on the new object.

The library thus has a reference now on the newly created object l. Note that, as the message for creation always returns a reference on the new object, we do not show the return explicitly, even though this is correct. We might obtain a more dense representation, such as that which is illustrated by the following figure.

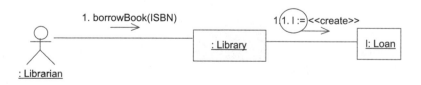

Figure 8.7 Collaboration diagram of the *borrowBook* operation (alternative continuation)

Let's continue our train of thought. Could the *date* and *returnDate* attributes not be set by the object l from its creation, following retrieval of the current date by a method that we will only explain in detail in detailed design?

This is what we are illustrating on the following collaboration diagram.

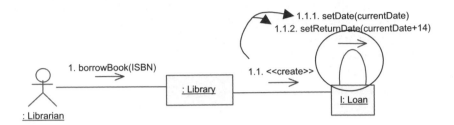

Figure 8.8 Collaboration diagram of the *borrowBook* operation (continuation 2)

Once again, notice (cf. Chapter 7) the use of decimal notation for the numbers of messages, which enables nested messages to be represented. We will also take note of the use of the loop above the object, which symbolises a link from the object to itself, as a medium through which a message "to oneself" is expressed.

The corresponding sequence diagram (with the notion of "focus of control") is given below by way of comparison.

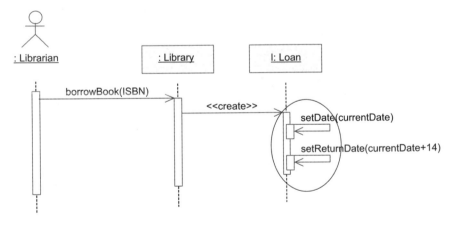

Figure 8.9 Sequence diagram of the *borrowBook* operation (continuation 2)

Let's go back to establishing the operation contract. What do we have to do now? We need a link with the book, whose ISBN attribute equals the ISBN that is passed as parameter of the *borrowBook* operation.

Which object is in the best position for finding a book according to its ISBN?

Let's go back to the analysis class diagram (Figure 8.2): the *Catalogue* class is the ideal candidate, as the catalogue knows all the books. But which object will send it the message? According to our collaboration diagram, it will be either the loan l, or the library.

In order to respect the principle of low coupling, it is better for the library to take care of it, as – contrary to the loan – it already possesses an association with the catalogue. Moreover, it is highly likely that the library will have to collaborate with the catalogue within the framework of other system operations, for example when adding new books. The library must therefore have a permanent link with the catalogue, which is definitely not the case of the loan. All these reasons clearly tip the scales favourably towards the library.

We will note that this assumes the catalogue and library objects are created at the time of initialising the system, and that a visibility link is established between them. In object-oriented design, it is common practice to work first on the collaborations between "business" objects, then secondly, deal with the more technical problem of initialising the information system. This enables a guarantee of the right decisions – with regard to assigning responsibilities to objects within the context of business collaborations – forcing initialisation and not the opposite.

Let's go back to our choice of communication between the library and the catalogue. What do we call the message? Let's call it *searchForBook*, with an ISBN number as parameter, and a reference *book* on the correct book object for the return.

The modified collaboration diagram is shown below.

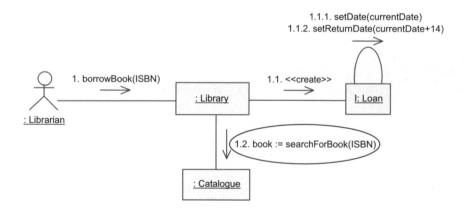

Figure 8.10 Collaboration diagram of the *borrowBook* operation (continuation 3)

What happens if the catalogue does not manage to find a book whose ISBN corresponds to the one that is being searched for? Is it not better to wait until we have this reference *book* before carrying out the creation of the loan l?

That's exactly it, and to do this, we simply have to change round the order of the two messages, as shown on the following figure. We will see that the decimal numbering of messages for assigning attributes is updated as a result.

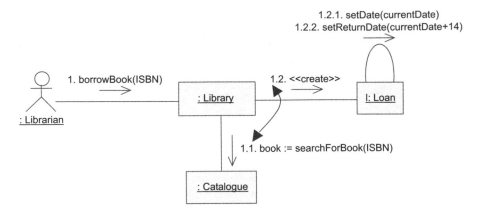

Figure 8.11 Collaboration diagram of the *borrowBook* operation (corrected continuation 3)

On the class diagram, there is a "1 - *" association between *Catalogue* and *Book*. This implies that the catalogue is going to use a collection of book objects, probably implemented in Java in the form of a *HashMap*. We have already listed the rules for expressing multiplicities of associations in Java collections in the preceding chapter (Figure 7.46). In Chapter 7, we also explained the use of the concept of "multiobject" in collaboration diagrams in order to rightly avoid making detailed design decisions too early (see Figure 7.18). This is the solution that we are also going to adopt here, with a more generic message than *searchForBook*, as the multiobject represents a technical object, "on the shelves", and not a "business" object.

The collaboration diagram is completed as follows.

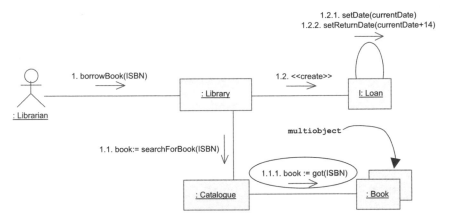

Figure 8.12 Collaboration diagram of the *borrowBook* operation (continuation 4)

Now that we have located the right book and that its reference has been returned to the library, we can make use of it to establish the link between the book and the loan. The most immediate solution entails passing the book reference as a parameter to the message for creation, as shown below.

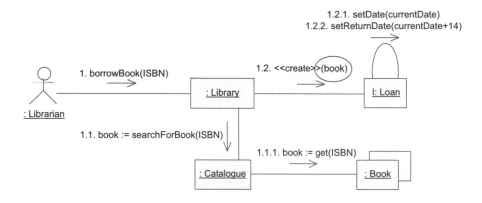

Figure 8.13 Collaboration diagram of the *borrowBook* operation (continuation 5)

Let's go back to the list of postconditions that need verifying, this time indicating the corresponding number from the preceding collaboration diagram:

- a loan l has been created: 1.2

- the *date* attribute of l has been set to the current date: 1.2.1

- the *returnDate* of l has been set to (the current date + two weeks): 1.2.2

- l has been linked to the book whose ISBN attribute equals the ISBN attribute passed as parameter: 1.1 and 1.2

- l has been linked to the member concerned and to the library: we still have to do this.

We therefore have to realise the last postcondition. Which object may know the member concerned? And furthermore, when has the system identified the member?

Let's remember that we are currently dealing with the *borrowBook* system operation, but it has been preceded by *identifyBorrower*, as the following diagram reminds us.

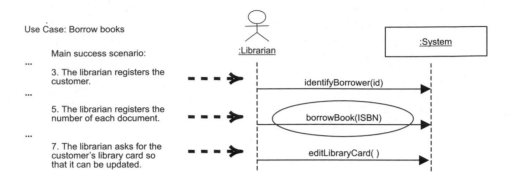

Figure 8.14 System operations of the *Borrow books* use case

It is therefore completely reasonable to think that, at the time of the *identifyBorrower* system operation, the library retained a reference on the member whilst processing. It can thus pass a reference on the member to the message for creation of the loan l.

The collaboration diagram now becomes:

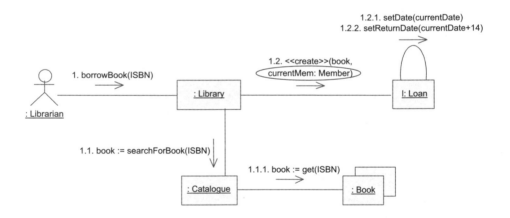

Figure 8.15 Collaboration diagram of the *borrowBook* operation (continuation 6)

The last postcondition also stipulates that a link has to exist between the library and the new loan l. As it is the library that creates l, the link already exists – at least transitorily. However, we can notice that a "1 - *" association exists between the *Library* and *Loan* classes, as is also the case between *Catalogue* and *Book*.

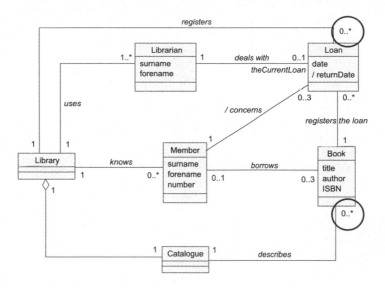

Figure 8.16 Analysis class diagram of the IS of the library

Now, which UML construction have we used in the case of the catalogue and of the books? A multiobject. Thus, by analogy, if the library wants to retain a permanent record of the loans that have been created, it needs a collection to which it must add the new loan l. As in Chapter 7 (cf. Figure 7.18), we will use a generic message, *add*(), to which we will pass into parameter the reference on the loan l.

The complete sequence and collaboration diagrams are shown in the following figures.

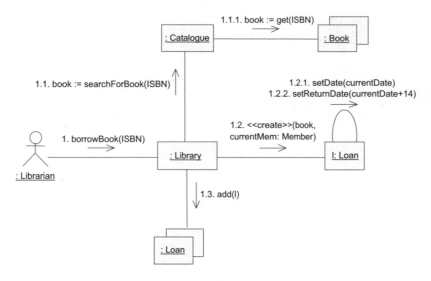

Figure 8.17 Complete collaboration diagram of the *borrowBook* operation

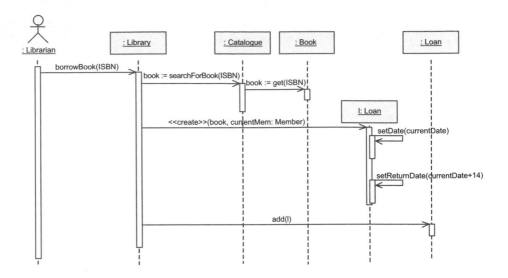

Figure 8.18 Complete sequence diagram of the *borrowBook* operation

*** 8.2 Propose a design class diagram that takes into account the results of the preceding question.

Answer 8.2

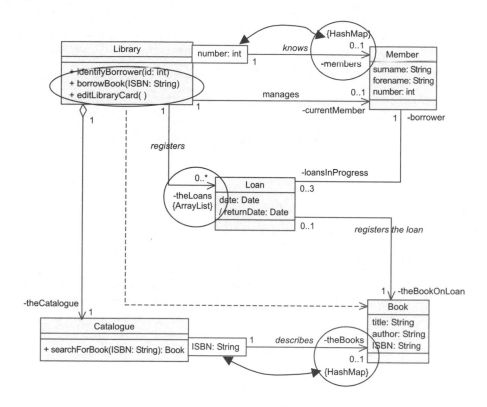

Figure 8.19 Design class diagram

With regard to the analysis class diagram (Figure 8.1), we can:

- add methods: the system operations processed by the *Library* class, but also *searchForBook* of the *Catalogue* class;

- define the type of attributes, as well as that of parameters and the return of methods;

- restrict the navigability of associations according to the direction of messages on links between objects of the collaboration diagram;

- specify the names of roles on the navigable side of associations, add qualifiers, as well as Java implementation recommendations for collections (for example {HashMap});

- remove unnecessary classes and associations in accordance with collaboration diagrams;

- add dependencies between classes further to temporary links between objects: *Library* depends on *Book* as it retrieves a reference on a book object, according to message 1.1 of the collaboration diagram.

** 8.3 Propose a Java skeleton code for the library class.

Fill in the body of the *borrowBook* method.

Answer 8.3

As we already explained in step 12 of Chapter 7, the transition of the class diagram to Java skeleton code, and that of the collaboration diagram to body of methods is quite straightforward. In this way, we easily obtain the following fragment of the "Library.java" file:

```
import java.user.*;

public class Library

{
    private Catalogue theCatalogue
    private Map members = new HashMap ( );
    private List theLoans = new ArrayList ( );
    private Member currentMember;

    public Library ( )
    {
        ...
    }

    public void identifyBorrower (int id)
    {
        ...
    }

    public void borrowBook (String ISBN)
    {
        Book book = theCatalogue.searchForBook (ISBN)  ;
        Loan l = new Loan (book, currentMember)  ;
        theLoans.add (l)  ;
    }

    public void editLibraryCard ( )
    {
        ...
    }

}
```

Figure 8.20 Java skeleton code of the *Library* class

Glossary & tips

This appendix comprises a thematic glossary of object-oriented design (mainly inspired by the one found in UML 2.0 Specifications from OMG), as well as a summary of tips, which have been taken from the two previous chapters.

Glossary

Architecture	Set of significant decisions relating to the organisation of a software system, the selection of structural elements that the system is made up of, and of their interfaces; as well as to their behaviour as it is specified in collaborations between these elements.
Collaboration	Specification of how an operation or classifier, such as a use case, is realized by a set of classifiers and associations playing specific roles used in a specific way. The collaboration defines an interaction.
Collection	Generic term that designates all object groupings without specifying the nature of the grouping.
Communication diagram (formerly collaboration diagram)	Diagram that focuses on the interaction between lifelines where the architecture of the internal structure and how this corresponds with the message passing is central. The sequencing of messages is given through a sequence numbering scheme. Sequence diagrams and communication diagrams express similar information, but show it in different ways.
Component	Modular part of a system that encapsulates its contents and whose manifestation is replaceable within its environment. A component defines its behaviour in terms of provided and required interfaces. As such, a component serves as a type, whose conformance is defined by these provided and reqiured interfaces (encompassing both their static as well as dynamic semantics).

Constructor	Class operation that constructs objects.
Controller	Artificial object that is introduced to separate the "Presentation" and "Business" software layers.
Coupling	1) Dependency between model elements. 2) "Coupling" represents a measure of the quantity of other classes, to which a given class is connected, which it knows about, or on which it depends.
Delegation	Ability of an object to issue a message to another object in response to a message. Delegation can be used as an alternative to inheritance.
Dependency	1) Obsolescence relationship between two model elements. 2) Semantic relationship between two elements, in which modification of one of the elements (the independent element) may have an effect on the semantics of the other element (the dependent element).
Deployment	Deployment shows the physical configuration of different run-time processing elements that take part in executing the system, as well as the component instances that they support.
Design	Phase of the system development process whose primary purpose is to decide how the system will be implemented. During design strategic and tactical decisions are made to meet the required functional and quality requirements of a system.
Inheritance	Mechanism by which more specific elements incorporate structure and behaviour of more general elements.
Implementation	Definition of how something is constructed or computed. For example, a class is an implementation of a type, a method is an implementation of an operation.
Importing	Dependency relationship between packages that make the public elements of a package visible within another package.
Interaction	Specification of how stimuli are sent between instances to perform a specific task. The interaction is defined in the context of a collaboration.
Interface	Named set of operations that characterise the behaviour of an element.

Layer
Organisation of classifiers or packages at the same level of abstraction. A layer may represent a horizontal slice through an architecture, whereas a partition represents a vertical slice.

Link
Semantic connection between objects, by which an object can communicate with another object by sending a message.

Logical architecture
1) In analysis: view of the architecture of a system comprising analysis classes, analysis packages and realisations of use cases; view which ultimately refines and structures the needs of the system.

2) In design: view of the architecture of a system comprising design classes, design subsystems, interfaces and realisations of use cases, which constitute the vocabulary of the field of the system solution.

Message
Specification of the conveyance of information from one instance to another, with the expectation that activity will ensue. A message may specify the raising of a signal or the call of an operation.

Method
Implementation of an operation. It specifies the algorithm or procedure associated with an operation.

Multiplicity
A specification of the range of allowable cardinalities that a set may assume. Multiplicity specifications may be given for association ends, parts within composites, repetitions, and other purposes. Essentially a multiplicity is a (possibly infinite) subset of the non-negative integers.

Multiobject
UML construction that represents several objects of the same class in a single symbol (particularly in a collaboration diagram). This prevents premature addition of detailed design classes, which are linked to the programming language.

Navigability
Quality of an association that allows navigation from one class to the other in a given direction.

Node
Classifier that represents a run-time computational resource, which generally has at least memory and often processing capability. Run-time objects and components may reside on nodes.

Object
Entity with well-defined boundaries, which is formed from a state, a behaviour and an identity; an object is an instance of a class.

Operation	Behavioural element of objects, which is defined globally in the class. Specification of a method.
Operation contract	Description of changes in state of the system when a system operation is invoked. These modifications are expressed in terms of "postconditions", which explain in detail the new state of the system after execution of the operation.
Package	General-purpose mechanism for organising elements in UML into groups, which can, for example, be used to group classes and associations.
Parameter	Argument of a behavioural feature. A parameter specifies arguments that are passed into or out of an invocation of a behavioural element like an operation. A parameter's type restricts what values can be passed.
Partition	Set of related classifiers or packages at the same level of abstraction or across layers in a layered architecture. A partition represents a vertical slice through an architecture, whereas a layer represents a horizontal slice.
Pattern	Recurrent and documented modelling solution, which can be applied in a given context.
Postcondition	Constraint which expresses a condition that must be true at the completion of an operation.
Precondition	Constraint which expresses a condition that must be true when an operation is invoked.
Private	Invisible from the exterior of a class (or of a package).
Public	Visible from the exterior of a class (or of a package).
Qualifier	Association attribute or tuple of attributes whose values partition the set of objects related to an object across an association.
Relationship	Abstact concept that specifies some kind of connection between elements. Examples of relationships include associations and generalisations.
Role	Name given to an association end: by extension, way in which the instances of a class see the instances of another class through an association.

Sequence diagram	Diagram that depicts an interaction by focusing on the sequence of messages that are exchanged, along with their corresponding event occurrences on the lifelines. Unlike a communication diagram, a sequence diagram includes time sequences but does not include object relationships. Sequence diagrams and communication diagrams express similar information, but show it in different ways.
Signature	Name and parameters of a behavioural feature. A signature may include optional returned parameter.
Stereotype	Class that defines how an existing metaclass (or stereotype) may be extended, and enables the use of platform or domain specific terminology or notation in addition to the ones used for the extended metaclass. Certain stereotypes are predefined in the UML, others may be user defined. Stereotypes are one of the extensibility mechanisms in UML.
System operation	Behaviour of system level, triggered by a message coming from an actor (by analogy with an operation at object level, triggered by receipt of a message coming from another object).
Visibilty	Enumeration whose value (public, protected, or private) denotes how the model element to which it refers may be seen outside its enclosing namespace.

Tips

- Separate your application into layers. The main reason for implementing 3-tier architecture is to isolate the business logic from presentation classes (GUI), as well as to ban direct access to data stored by these presentation classes. The primary concern is to meet the criterion of flexibility: to be able to modify the interface of the application without having to modify the business rules, and being able to change storage mechanism without having to adapt the interface or the business rules.

- To improve modularity, insert an artificial object called a "controller" between the graphical objects and the business objects. This design object knows the interface of objects of the business layer and plays the role of "façade" with regard to the presentation layer.

- In simple cases, the controller can be an object of an existing analysis class:

  - either an object representing the whole system or the organisation itself;

- or an object representing a role that would have realised the system operation.

- Describe your layered architecture by using a static diagram that only shows packages and their dependencies. You can use the « `layer` » predefined stereotype to distinguish the packages that represent layers.

- Do not forget that the analysis/design process is a fundamentally iterative one. The preliminary architecture may be refined or modified (mainly at the level of partitions within each layer) by the design work that will follow the first analysis division.

- Use operation contracts: these enable the link to be made between the functional/dynamic view of use cases and the analysis static view. An operation contract describes changes in state of the system when a system operation is invoked. These changes are expressed in terms of "postconditions", which explain in detail the new state of the system after execution of the operation. The main postconditions concern the creation (or destruction) of objects and links descended from the analysis static model, as well as the modification of attribute values.

- Use the standard textual description plan for an operation contract given below:

  - name

  - responsibilities

  - references

  - preconditions

  - postconditions

  - exceptions (optional)

  - notes (optional)

- Design system operations, respecting their chronology.

- To progress from the analysis to the design stage, use the three Jacobson stereotypes that enable graphical representation of how a message sent by an actor traverses the business, application and presentation layers:

- <<boundary>>: classes that are used to model the interactions between the system and its actors;

- <<control>>: classes used to represent the coordination, sequence and control of other objects – in general, they are linked to a specific use case;

- <<entity>>: classes that are used to model long-lived and often persistent information.

- On collaboration diagrams, use decimal numbering which allows overlapping of messages to be shown, in a way comparable to the representation of "focus of control" on the sequence diagram.

- Do not forget that postconditions only represent the new state of the system once the system operation has completed its execution. They are certainly not ordered: it is the role of the designer to choose which object must realise each action, and in what order.

- Take system operations as your starting point for initialising your dynamic study in the form of collaboration diagrams.

- The sequence diagram becomes increasingly difficult to read as objects are added. It is for this simple reason that the collaboration diagram is essential for design: it enables objects to be placed in both dimensions, thereby improving the readability of the diagram. The collaboration diagram possesses another advantage over the sequence diagram: it also allows the representation of structural relationships among objects.

- In your collaboration diagrams, use the UML construction of "multiobject". This prevents a detailed design class that is linked to the programming language, such as *Vector* of the STL C++ or *ArrayList* in Java, etc. from being added too soon.

- An interesting idea for improving the readability of the collaboration diagram entails dividing it into two by treating the controller object as a transition marker:

  - one part to specify the kinematics of the human-computer interface with the actors, the <<boundary>> objects and the <<control>> object;

  - a second part to specify the dynamics of the application and business layers with the <<control>> object and the <<entity>> objects.

- To start with, work on the collaborations between "business" objects, then deal with the more technical problem of initialising the information system. This enables a guarantee of the right decisions, with regard to assigning responsibilities to objects within the context of business collaborations, forcing initialisation, and not the opposite.

- Collaboration diagrams will allow development of design class diagrams, and this is done by adding mainly the following information to classes from the analysis model:

  - operations: a message can only be received by an object if its class has declared the corresponding public operation;

  - the navigability of associations or dependencies between classes, according to whether links between objects are long-lasting or temporary, and according to the direction in which messages are circulating.

- Be careful: a long-lasting link between objects will give rise to a navigable association between corresponding classes; a temporary link (by parameter: « parameter », or local variable: « local ») will give rise to a simple dependency relationship. Do not add the classes that correspond to multiobjects in the design class diagram. This is so that they remain independent from the target programming language for as long as possible.

- With regard to messages of collaboration diagrams, do not show the following in design class diagrams:

  - creation operations (<<create>> message),

  - generic operations on the container classes (*add*(), etc.),

  - operations for accessing attributes.

- You can use the « parameter » and « local » stereotypes on dependencies between class, in order to mirror the type of temporary link that exists between the corresponding objects in the collaboration diagram.

- Retaining low coupling is a principle that you must always aim to respect for all design decisions; it is an underlying objective, which is to be assessed continuously. Indeed, by catering for it, we generally obtain a more flexible application that is easier to maintain.

- In addition, do not forget to show in the class diagram those that do not belong to the current package. It is important to show their relationships with classes of the current package to justify then the direction of dependencies between the incorporated packages. In fact, we should only represent the navigable associations, the dependencies or generalisations, which point at classes that are external to those of the package concerned.

- In order to represent a logical architecture visually and in detail, all you have to do is make a list of all the classes used in the different diagrams, and represent them graphically within the appropriate package.

- UML design models enable the simple production of code in an object-oriented programming language, such as Java:

  - class diagrams enable the description of the skeleton code, i.e. all the declarations;

  - collaboration diagrams allow the body of methods to be written, particularly the sequence of method calls on objects that interact.

- Our first approach:

  - the UML class becomes a Java class;

  - UML attributes become Java instance variables;

  - methods that enable read (get) and write (set) access to attributes, in order to respect the principle of encapsulation, are implicit;

  - UML operations become Java methods;

  - navigable roles produce instance variables, just like attributes, but with a user type instead of a simple type;

  - the constructor is implicit by default.

- Do not forget import statements for relationships with classes that belong to other packages, as well as for basic Java classes.

- How do we translate navigable associations of "*" multiplicity? Use a reference attribute pointing to a collection instance, which contains in turn instances of the many-side class. The difficulty consists in choosing the right collection among the many basic classes that Java offers. Although it is possible to create arrays in Java, this is not necessarily the right solution. On this subject, we prefer instead to resort to collections, among which the ones that are used most often are *ArrayList* (formerly *Vector*) and *HashMap* (formerly *HashTable*). Use *ArrayList* if you have to respect a specific order and retrieve objects from an integer index; use *HashMap* if you wish to retrieve objects from an arbitrary key.

- Describe the physical implementation of your application by using the last two types of diagram offered by UML:

  - the component diagram;

  - the deployment diagram.

- Use the component diagram to show specific dependencies among the software components that constitute the application. If possible, give details of the interfaces of components and link the dependencies to the interfaces, rather than to the components themselves.

- Use the deployment diagram to show the physical configuration of different run-time processing elements that take part in executing the system, as well as the component instances that they support. Be careful: the components that no longer exist at run-time do not appear on this diagram; these must be shown on component diagrams.

- Study the design patterns until you are just as familiar with them as you are with the basic object-oriented concepts!

Index